Unix for Users

COMPUTER SCIENCE TEXTS

COMPUTER SCIENCE TEXTS

Unix® for Users

CHRIS MILLER
MA, MPhil, Dip Comp Sci
Network Designers Ltd, Wetherby

ROGER BOYLE
BA, MPhil, MBCS
School of Computer Studies
University of Leeds

ANDREW STEWART
BSc, MBCS
Department of Computer Science
University of Hull

SECOND EDITION

OXFORD

BLACKWELL SCIENTIFIC PUBLICATIONS

LONDON EDINBURGH BOSTON

MELBOURNE PARIS BERLIN VIENNA

© 1984 by Blackwell Scientific
Publications
© 1990 by Chris Miller, Roger Boyle,
Andrew Stewart

Blackwell Scientific Publications
Editorial offices:
Osney Mead, Oxford OX2 0EL
25 John Street, London WC1N 2BL
23 Ainslie Place, Edinburgh EH3 6AJ
3 Cambridge Center, Suite 208
    Cambridge, Massachusetts 02142, USA
54 University Street, Carlton
    Victoria 3053, Austraila

First published 1984
Second edition 1990

Printed in Great Britain by
Billing & Sons Ltd, Worcester

Unix® is a trademark of A T & T.

DISTRIBUTORS

Marston Book Services Ltd
PO Box 87
Oxford OX2 0DT
(Orders: Tel: 0865 791155
         Fax: 0865 791927
         Telex: 837515

USA
Publishers' Business Services
PO Box 447
Brookline Village
Massachusetts 02147
(Orders: Tel (617) 524-7678)

Canada
Oxford University Press
70 Wynford Drive
Don Mills
Ontario M3C 1J9
(Orders: Tel (416) 441-2941)

Australia
Blackwell Scientific Publications
(Australia) Pty Ltd
54 University Street
Carlton, Victoria 3053
(Orders: Tel: (03) 347-0300)

British Library
Cataloguing in Publication Data
Miller, Chris
    Unix for users.—2nd ed.—(Computer
    science texts).
    1. Computer systems. Operating
    systems: UNIX
    I. Title   II. Boyle, Roger   III. Stewart,
    Andrew   IV. Series
    005.43

    ISBN 0-632-02416-X

Library of Congress
Cataloguing in Publication Data
Miller, Chris (Chris D. F.)
    Unix for users/Chris Miller, Roger
    Boyle, Andrew Stewart.—2nd ed.
        p. cm.—(Computer science texts)
        Includes bibliographical references.
        ISBN 0-632-02416-X
        1. UNIX (Computer operating
    system) I. Boyle, Roger.
    II. Stewart, Andrew.   III. Title.
    IV. Series.
    QA76.76.O63M56   1990

Contents

Preface to 2nd Edition

This book is not intended as a substitute for the Unix[1] Programmer's Manual. Indeed, it could not possibly be one, since the manuals provided with the Berkeley BSD4.3 and AT&T System V distributions run to a large number of volumes — approximately six and ten, respectively. To attempt to encapsulate all this information in one short book would be both unreasonable and superfluous.

Instead, we aim to provide an introduction to the complete novice which will at the same time be something more than an introduction, and will be of value to the experienced computer user who wants to know something about Unix. We hope that we have provided a basis for intelligent exploration and understanding of the appropriate areas of the Programmer's Manual.

The beginner will find some chapters substantially more demanding than others. In particular, the chapter on the system interfaces presupposed some knowledge of, and experience with, the language C, although even without such knowledge it can be read to give an idea of the architecture of the system. The chapter on systems maintenance may also be beyond the scope of the average beginner, although with the advent of Unix on personal computers it is becoming increasingly relevant. It is perfectly possible to omit these more advanced chapters at a first reading, and still obtain enough understanding of the system to make effective use of it.

We have chosen to describe both the Berkeley and AT&T distributions of Unix, since the vast majority of modern Unix systems are descended from one or other of these systems. In general we provide a generic description, pointing out features and differences as they become important. Most of the discussion is, however, relevant to most systems that claim to be "Unix-like".

We should like to acknowledge the Department of Computer Studies at Leeds University for providing the environment in which the first edition of this book was written, and the Department of Computer Science

---

[1]Unix is a registered trademark of AT&T in the U.S.A and other countries.

at the University of Hull for the environment in which this, the second edition, was prepared.

Any errors of fact are the joint responsibility of all the authors; any errors of typography are the responsibility of Andrew Stewart or Roger Boyle. Jointly, they will be glad to incorporate any corrections into future editions.

Roger Boyle
University of Leeds
Chris Miller
Network Designers Ltd.
Andrew Stewart
University of Hull

April, 1990

Chapter 1

Getting Started

This chapter is intended as an introduction both for those who have never used a computer system before, and for those who are more experienced but have not encountered Unix previously; the latter will probably want to skip much of the general introductory material which follows.

1.1 WHAT IS UNIX?

Unix is a computer operating system, developed at Bell Laboratories in the United States. If that description has already left you behind, then you probably want to know ...

What Is An Operating System?

If a computer system consisted of nothing more than the bare "hardware" — chips, wires, printed circuits, disk drives, terminals, and so on — it would be virtually impossible for anyone but an expert to make use of it. There are two main reasons for this.

The first is that the computer obeys instructions written in a highly arcane language known as *machine code*, a language which varies from one model of computer to another. Programming in machine code is a specialised and dying art, because of the widespread availability of numerous *high-level programming languages*, which make it possible for computer users to express solutions to their problems as computer programs in terms much closer to those in which the problems were originally formulated. Although we shall briefly discuss some aspects of one high-level language, C, later in the book (Chapter 9), and will mention various others, this book is not about computer programming, and we will assume that if you are not already familiar with the concept of programming, you are pursuing the topic elsewhere.

The second difficulty in using a naked computer is that the hardware provides many services — access to peripheral devices such as disks and terminals, timing, storage protection — in a form which is far too primitive for the average user to make effective use of them. To make them more accessible, most computers run a program known as the *operating system* that presents the machine's services to a user and to her programs in a form that makes them easier to use. The operating system (often abbreviated in computing literature to *OS*) fulfils many functions, which typically include some or all of:

- organising the storage space on devices such as disks, floppy disks, and magnetic tapes into logical units, usually known as *files*, where information can be stored and later retrieved;

- providing a simple interface for programs to transmit information to and from external devices;

- providing information such as the time of day;

- managing the simultaneous execution of several programs;

- providing facilities whereby simultaneously executing programs can communicate information to one another.

- providing facilities for users and programs on one system to communicate with users and programs on another, either locally or at a distance.

The ability to run simultaneous programs is known as *time-sharing*. In fact, on most systems today programs do not truly run simultaneously; rather, the computer devotes its attention to each in turn for a short span of time, thus sharing out its total computing power amongst them. Having said this, there is a steady increase in the number of commercially available *Parallel Computers*, where programs can truly run simultaneously. A number of these machines support Unix in one form or another. If properly managed, time-sharing can lead to a far more efficient use of the machine, since frequently a program will stop, waiting for some external event such as data arriving from a terminal, and it would be wasteful to have the entire computer grind to a halt under such circumstances.

A common form of time-sharing is a *multi-user* system; in such a system several users can sit at different terminals, all sharing the resources of a single computer, but each user seeing it as, in effect, her own private machine. The only way in which one user is normally affected by the presence of other users is that if there are too many, it may seem as though her personal machine is running more slowly than usual.

Operating systems range in size from the very small systems which run on many microcomputers, often providing no more than the language BASIC, communication with the terminal, and simple file-handling on cassette and floppy disk, to the giant behemoths which run on the large *mainframe* computers, providing simultaneous access to tens or hundreds of users, and offering a vast panoply of services. In this spectrum, it is hard to say exactly where Unix fits in; in some aspects it is a "small" system — it is available on many microcomputers and personal machines, and is well suited to a small machine; on the other hand, it offers a large collection of support programs, will handle many simultaneous users, and is available on many medium-sized and large computers. Thus we are brought back to our original question ...

1.2   WHAT IS UNIX?

Unix is a time-sharing operating system; it was originally released as a multi-user system, but there are now many single-user computers which run it; there is naturally no problem in using a multi-user system to serve a single user. Unix, like most other operating systems, is divided into two separate parts: the *kernel*, which is the program which most precisely fits the description of operating systems which we have given above, and the *utilities*, a large collection of programs which carry out a wide range of useful tasks. The utilities are what most users of the system actually perceive to be the greater part of Unix; the services provided by the kernel are normally of relevance only to those who will be writing high-level language programs intended to run on Unix systems (and nowhere else). However, in the strictest sense, Unix consists *only* of the kernel; it is perfectly possible to equip the kernel with an entirely different set of utilities, changing the outward appearance of the system altogether, and still have a Unix system; although this is occasionally done in tailoring Unix for particular applications, we shall usually use the term *Unix* in the looser sense, meaning the kernel and the "standard" set of utilities which are distributed as part of almost all Unix systems.

We shall discuss some aspects of the kernel and the services it provides to the programmer in Chapter 9, although unfortunately the detailed workings of the system are protected by licensing agreements which pre-

vent us from entering into too much detail about the way in which Unix
has been designed and written. [1] Most of the rest of the book is occupied
with describing those utilities which you are most likely to meet, or which
are of particular intrinsic interest, together with a general introduction to
the use of Unix as an interactive operating system, and a description of
essential concepts such as *files*.

Unix By Any Other Name

Although we have used the name *Unix* to describe the topic of our book,
and shall continue to do so, there are in fact a number of different flavours
of Unix, under an assortment of brand-names. It is probably worthwhile
at this point to clarify which systems we are talking about, and issue a
few warnings about possible differences between one Unix and another.

There are three different kinds of system which can loosely be regarded as either Unix or Unix-like: "true" Unixes, re-writes of Unix, and
Unix emulations; most of what we say in this book will apply equally to
all three.

True Unixes are versions which consist mostly or entirely of one of
the original versions of Unix from Bell Laboratories (or one of their related companies), perhaps modified to run on different hardware from
the original version. For the most part, these systems will have the same
commands and utilities as we describe in this book (but heed the warnings
below about the various different releases). Amongst such systems are
Unix Version 7, *Unix System III*, *Unix System V*, *Berkeley Unix*, *SUNOS*,
Xenix, *Omnix*, and *UniFlex*.

Unix re-writes are complete re-implementations of Unix from the bottom up; they are not generally covered by the same licensing arrange-
ments as the true Unixes, and may provide a different (usually more
restricted) collection of commands. Furthermore, the actual command
names may be different, and the way in which they are used also varies
somewhat. Among these systems are *Idris*, *MINIX*, *MACH*, and *GNU*.
One of the intentions of the recently-formed *Open Software Foundation*
is to produce a complete re-implementation of Unix. There are also several claimants to the title of "Unix-like system" which are, frankly, too
far removed from Unix to deserve the name.

---

[1]For the incurably curious and strong of heart, see [4] for an excellent description of
the Unix kernel.

Unix emulations are environments provided within another operating system; usually they make use of the original Unix versions of the utility programs, but may provide only a restricted collection of the low-level services of the Unix kernel. In some cases (such as Amdahl's *UTS*) it is rather difficult to know whether to classify a system as a true Unix or an emulation; of course, where such an emulation is successful it scarcely matters anyway. In addition to *UTS*, which runs within the *VM470* operating system, there are *Eunice* and *Unity*, both of which run within *VMS* on Digital Equipment Corporation's *VAX* series of computers. The emergence of the *POSIX*, *X/Open* and *SVID* interface standards will probably result in Unix-like emulations appearing on a wide range of computer systems.

In most respects, this book should be helpful for any of the flavours of Unix which you are likely to encounter. However, the face of Unix is changing so rapidly at the moment that differences between versions are inevitable, and will sometimes be quite large; in particular, with the gradual merging of the Berkeley and AT&T versions of Unix, many features will depend upon the origin of your Unix system and the manufacturer of your computer. We will try to point out the differences that you are likely to find as we go on, but to avoid enumerating a dozen exceptions every time that we mention a feature we will list some of the main differences in the remainder of this chapter.

Talking To The Computer

If you have access to a computer running Unix, you are presumably by now wondering, perhaps a little impatiently, when we are going to get round to telling you how to use it. In case you have never used any computer system before, we shall try to start at the very beginning; however, just as a picture is worth a thousand words, so also a helping hand is worth a thousand pictures. If you are able to find an experienced user to hold your hand through these first stages, it will all become very easy very quickly; if all you have to hand is this book, then life will probably, sadly, be a little harder.

The first thing to learn is how to use a *terminal*. Unix is primarily an *interactive* system, in which you enter commands at a terminal and receive the results there in response. The terminal is nowadays usually a television-type screen with an attached keyboard, generally known as a *VDU* (visual display unit) or *CRT* (cathode-ray tube), although it may also be a printer of some kind with a keyboard (a *hard-copy* terminal). If your terminal has both capital letters and lower-case, then the very first thing to do when talking to Unix is to *make sure that the shift lock* (or *'alpha lock'* or *'capitals lock'*) *is OFF*. Unix usually interacts in lower-case, and users with capitals-only terminals, such as old-fashioned teletypes, will have an uncomfortable time of it.

When typing at the terminal, there are several useful keys which will cause things to happen, or will enable you to correct mistakes in your typing.

Control Characters

Before we explain what these useful keys do, a small piece of notation: several 'special' characters on Unix are *control characters*. These are typed by *holding down* the key labelled CONTROL (or CTRL), and typing some other character while CONTROL is still depressed (in exactly the same way that the SHIFT key is used on both terminals and conventional typewriters). Rather than laboriously write out 'control-U' every time that we mean "hold down CONTROL and press U", there is a very common convention which we shall use throughout the rest of the book: whenever we mean "control-U" we shall write ^U, and similarly ^C for "control-C", and so on. On some keyboards, there may be a key which is also labelled with the character "↑", although it is more commonly labelled "^"; to avoid all ambiguity we shall always write this character as "^". (Thus ↑^will mean "hold down CONTROL and type ^").

Special Keys - RETURN

The most important special key is the one labelled RETURN (or ENTER or CARRIAGE RETURN or CR on some keyboards). Usually, no command that you enter will be executed by Unix until you type a RETURN at the end of your command line. This simple point cannot be stressed enough — almost every beginner in computing has at some time typed in a command, and then spent the next few minutes staring at an unresponding terminal, wondering "Why isn't it doing anything?" The answer, almost invariably is "because you didn't end the line with RETURN!". Even if you read this paragraph five times, it can still happen to you (and probably will despite all the warnings).

Local Line-Editing

Few of us are perfect typists, and so we occasionally make typing errors when entering a line to the system. Fortunately, it is possible to undo the error if it is spotted in time; this is done by various *local line-editing* keys on the terminal. These are the CHARACTER-DELETE, LINE-DELETE, and (on some systems) WORD-DELETE keys — but don't look for them on your keyboard yet. It is a regrettable fact that different Unixes use different keys for these line-editing functions, and you will have to find out what they are on your particular system. Having said this, Unix does provide a command that allows you to change many of the editing keys to suit yourself; you will find a brief description of this command on page 122. The most common choices for CHARACTER-DELETE are: RUBOUT (often labelled DELETE) and BACKSPACE (often labelled ←); the most common choice for LINE-DELETE is ^U; when word-delete is available, it is usually ^W.

Because of the profusion of possible characters for the line-editing functions, we shall adopt our own symbols, which you may translate into whatever is appropriate for your system. We shall write CHARACTER-DELETE as ©and LINE-DELETE as ⓛ, and WORD-DELETE as ⓦ.

Let us see a few examples. If you type

```
This has shome©©©©ome mish©takes.
```

then the line which will be seen by Unix when you type RETURN will be

```
This has some mistakes.
```

If you type

```
This line is a complete disast!?*#%&"!&%ⓛForget it.
```

then Unix will only see

```
Forget it.
```

What will actually appear on your screen when you type the character- and line-delete characters varies from one system to another; on most systems using visual display terminals the erased text will actually disappear from the screen as you rub it out, while on others deleted characters may appear one by one sandwiched between backslashes, thus:

```
This has shome©\emoh©/ome mish©\h©/takes.
```

Although you will no doubt quickly become used to the habits of your own system in this respect it is worth remembering that many of these editing characters can be tailored to suit you.

Other Characters

There are three other special characters which you need to know from an early stage.

The first of these is the END-OF-FILE character. Many programs recognise this as marking the end of input from the terminal; a very important special case of this is that the *shell*, which is the program which reads your commands from the terminal and executes them, will recognise the end-of-file character as a sign that you have finished your current session of using Unix, and would like to *log off*. (If you attempt to log off and receive the message

```
Use ''logout'' to leave csh
```

you are using the *C-shell* with the shell variable *ignoreeof* set. For further information on C-shell variables, see page 100. In the meantime you can log off by typing `logout`.) On a multi-user system it is important to log off from the system whenever you have finished using it, both to protect any of your own information on the system — if you do not log off someone else might use the terminal you have left logged on to impersonate you and destroy or gain access to information which you want to keep secure — and also to leave your terminal free for others to use (if it is publicly accessible).

The keyboard character used for end-of-file varies from system to system; on many systems in Europe, it will be ^Z; on most others it will be ^D. Like the line editing characters, the end-of-file character can be changed, although doing so can cause great confusion. To avoid confusion we will use the symbol © to represent this character.

The final two special characters are INTERRUPT and QUIT. It will occasionally happen that after you have started something going on the system, you decide subsequently that you would rather not wait for it to finish. It may also happen that you have written a program on the system which has gone into an infinite loop. In either of these cases, you can type the INTERRUPT character, which asks Unix to abandon its current

Special Keyboard Characters		
Character	**Symbol**	**Common Possibilities**
Character delete	ⓒ	BACKSPACE, RUBOUT
Line delete	ⓛ	^U, ^X
Word delete	ⓦ	^W
End of file	ⓔ	^Z, ^D
Interrupt	ⓘ	^C, RUBOUT, BREAK
Quit	^\	^\

Table 1.1: Special Keyboard Characters

activity on your behalf, and to accept further commands from your terminal; most programs, when interrupted, will die and go away completely, but a few (such as the file-editor) will take some other action. Just occasionally (usually with a program which you yourself have written which tries to handle INTERRUPT cleverly), INTERRUPT will not achieve the result you want; in almost all such cases, the QUIT character *will* do so (usually with the message "Quit - core dumped" printed out at you). The file produced by a "core dump" can be quite large — it is usually called *core*, and you should take care to remove it using the *rm* command. Thus QUIT can be seen as a more drastic form of INTERRUPT.

On every Unix system we know of, the keyboard QUIT character is ^\; the interrupt character varies, but is almost always one of ^C or RUBOUT (which may alternatively be labelled DELETE); the key labelled BREAK will usually have the same effect as well.

For a table summarising the special keyboard characters, see Table 1.1.

A Note About Pausing Output

On a VDU, output has an unpleasant habit of arriving on your screen much faster than you can read it; worse, as output arrives at the bottom of the screen, earlier output *scrolls* off the top, and disappears forever. There are three solutions which different Unix systems offer to this.

The first, found on some installations, is for Unix to cope with the problem directly. At the end of each screenful of output, the system will automatically pause, and wait for you to type any character before it sends the next screenful. If the character you type is a ^P, this automatic pausing is turned off.

The second is to provide a special program which performs the same function; if you want output to pause every screenful, you have to direct it through this program (usually using a *pipeline*, described in the chapter on the Shell). One such program is *more*, from the University of California at Berkeley; another example is *pg*, in System V.

The third possibility, which is almost always available even on systems offering one or other of the first two, is to leave matters entirely in your hands. You can stop output at any time by typing a *stop* character, almost invariably ^S, and can resume it again by typing a *start* character, almost invariably ^Q. (Some Unix systems will accept any character as a start character — like many terminal features, this can often be configured to suit the user.)

1.3 LOGGING ON TO UNIX

Once again, we are in an area where different systems vary from one another; in case you are beginning to despair, rest assured that most of the material after this chapter applies equally to all versions of Unix; it is the area of terminal handling which is by far the most variable of all Unix features, and once over this initial hurdle life becomes much easier.

Usernames

To use Unix (and most other multi-user systems), you need to tell the system who you are. You do this so that you may have proper access to the information on the system which belongs to you, and to prevent other users from tampering with it, either maliciously or accidentally.

The way that you identify yourself is by a *username*; on a multi-user system, you will be given a username when you first obtain authorisation to use the system, while on a single-user personal system you should receive instructions with your system on how to set it up initially. In addition to a username, you will need a *password*; this is a secret word which (ideally) only you know, and which prevents other people from logging in with your username to impersonate you. At some installations users are initially set up with no password, at others the password will start out the same as the username, at still others you will be asked to specify what password you would like when you are first authorised to use the system; you should consult the local authorities for guidance. No matter what your password is to start with, you should change it to one of your own choosing as soon as possible, and change it fairly frequently thereafter. We shall describe how to do this in Section 2.5.

Logging In

In almost all systems, the first step of logging in is to find a terminal which is displaying the message [2]

```
login:
```

possibly preceded by some system identification, thus:

```
University of Hull S81 - Berkeley Unix
login:
```

You should seek out your local systems administrator for help with finding a free terminal that you can use, and for information about your local network; the following general advice, however, may be of some help. If you find a vacant terminal which is instead displaying some other message or a blank screen, then you should:

1. Make sure that no-one else is using the terminal; they will be justifiably irritated if they return from a momentary absence to find that you have usurped them!

2. If the terminal is genuinely free, type an end-of-file; this should cause anyone currently logged in to be logged out, and will probably result in the login message being displayed.

3. If by some chance the required response does not materialise, try typing the interrupt character, followed by an end-of-file; a further possibility is to try the quit character, followed by end-of-file.

4. It may be that the terminal responds by displaying obvious gibberish. The cause of this is usually that Unix has the wrong idea about the speed at which to send data to the terminal, and the usual cure

---

[2] In this and all subsequent displays of what you should see on a terminal, we show computer output in **boldface**, and what the user types in roman.

is repeatedly to type BREAK followed by RETURN; each time you do this, Unix should try a different speed, eventually coming up with the right one.

5. If all the above fails, then try to find either a different terminal or a local expert; there is probably something wrong, or significantly different about your Unix system.

Warning — *do not* try the following suggestion unless the instructions with your system explicitly tell you to do so; you may lose valuable data if you reload the system at the wrong time!

For single-user systems running on microcomputers, it may be possible to get the login message by switching the computer off and on again, or by pressing the REBOOT switch or its equivalent.

Let us assume that by now you have obtained the "login: " message. The system is now waiting for you to type your *username*.

When Unix invites you to *login:*, you should respond by typing your username (followed by RETURN); then, if you have a password, Unix will respond with the line

`Password:`

in response to which you should type your password; do not be surprised when what you type does not appear on the terminal — this is Unix's way of helping to keep your password a secret. If you typed your username and password correctly, you have now succeeded in *logging on* (or *logging in* — the terms are generally used interchangeably) to Unix, and should receive a *prompt* indicating that Unix is waiting for you to type commands at it, perhaps preceded by a few "messages of the day" and other useful information. On most systems the prompt is the character *$* (dollar), although on some it may be *%* if you are using the C-Shell, or the word *READY*, or indeed almost anything else. Thus the entire process of logging in will appear on your terminal as something like:

```
University of Hull S81 - Berkeley Unix
login:  chris
password:
The system will be going down at 11.00 for
1 hour for preventive maintenance

You have mail
$
```

What happens next is the substance of most of the rest of this book!

Logging Off

One last reminder before we move on to an introduction to Unix commands: you should always remember to *log off* when you have finished a session. This is normally done by typing the end-of-file character, ⓒ; on a few systems you may have to type an explicit command such as *logout* or *exit*. If you encounter the message

```
There are stopped jobs
```

then you are using the C-Shell; at this point, you can either

1. ignore the stopped jobs and type ⓒ or *logout* again — the stopped jobs will be removed and you will then be logged out.

2. study the chapter on the C-Shell, and in particular section 7.8, to recover the stopped jobs before logging out.

When you log off, some systems may respond by typing out a few statistics, such as how much computer time you used during your session; others, following the usual Unix philosophy of taciturnity, will simply print out a login message inviting another user to start a session.

One final word of warning — the laconic conciseness of Unix messages has become almost famous within the world of Operating Systems. If the error messages that you get from Unix seem a little obscure from time to time, don't worry — they will become clearer as you go on.

Chapter 2

Simple Commands

Unix thinks in **files**. A file is any collection of information you may think of as a logical unit, for example a shopping list, or a pile of experimental data, or some program you have written to analyse that data, or indeed the resulting compiled and linked "binary" program.

This interpretation of "file" is common to nearly all modern computer systems; words like *filestore* and *file system* have some sort of meaning whichever operating system you happen to be using and Unix is no exception. The other universal feature, of larger systems at any rate, is the presence of *peripheral devices*. At their simplest these are terminals (you are almost bound to need one of these), beyond which are lineprinters to give you hard copy output, magnetic tape drives used for long term storage and disks for on-line storage. Many systems will have further, more sophisticated devices. Whatever you have, a principal characteristic of your computer's operating system is the way it views its devices, and here Unix presents its first unique feature. In addition to the usual abstract interpretation of file, it also views each of its devices as a file. Thus a common activity is to "store a file" — this usually means that you deposit it on disk or tape somewhere; when Unix types out some data on your terminal, it considers that it is storing that information in the file represented by your terminal. Similarly when a file is printed on a lineprinter, that, to Unix, is storing it in the file represented by the lineprinter. A good Unix rule of thumb is "most things are files".

Perhaps this implies that Unix is a chaotic collection of files. This is of course not true; if no order or structure were to be imposed on our files, computing would be a disorganised and impossible task. In fact each file will have attributes of its own; in particular, each one will have its owner. It does remain true to say that the Unix design provides for a collection of people to own a collection of files, some of which are programs, some of which are physical devices, some of which are shopping lists, and so on, together with the mechanisms to move them around, duplicate them, throw them away, and indeed manipulate them in more or less any way you care to imagine.

16

Each file has a unique owner; usually, as you may expect, the owner will be the user who created the file, so that files concerned with system management will be owned by "The System" (user *root*) as will, generally, the files that represent devices such as lineprinters, disks and tape drives. Likewise, you will be able to own files of your own. These files will, by default, accumulate in your **login directory**, (also referred to as your *home directory*) which you may regard as your own work area. As a new user you may expect your login directory to appear empty when you first log in. In fact, as soon as you log on you already own one file — the terminal you sit at belongs to you until you log off the system.

2.1 CREATING A FILE

You can create your first file quite simply by using the Unix command *cat*. *cat* is an abbreviation for "catenate", and its action is to list the contents of one or more files into another one. We shall use the fact that Unix considers the terminal to be a file, and ask it to list the contents of the terminal (i.e. what we type on it) into a file which we shall name and store in the login directory. The command looks like this;

```
$ cat > file1
```

cat now takes whatever we type at the terminal and deposits it into a file which we have decided to call *file1*. Beware! it will continue so to do, divorcing you from the system and its "$" prompt, until you tell it that you have finished the file (or otherwise interrupt it). This is accomplished by entering the *End-of-File* character ⓔ. Thus the command, input and End-of-file sequence may look like

```
$ cat > file1
These few words are my first file
ⓔ
$
```

There is already one particularly important point to note. The file may be called nearly anything we please so long as the length of the name does not exceed some pre-defined limit. On Berkeley Unix systems, the limit is 255 characters; on Version 7 and System V, the limit is usually 14 characters. For example, the name *file1* could have been *fileone*, *file-one*, *first.file, 1-file* or *+@:#*. It is, however, good practice from everybody's point of view to use file names that reflect the contents of the file, and similarly good practice to restrict names to using "sensible" characters. Thus names like *+@:#* are cumbersome to use and rather bad as clues to the file's contents. Likewise we are able to use any of the control characters ^A, ^B, ...in filenames, but seldom do. Note, though, that we may use upper case letters if we choose, or a mixture of upper and lower, and Unix will know the difference. It is a common beginner's error not to appreciate that *File1* and *file1* are different names, as are *FILE1* and *filE1*.

Filenames normally refer to files in your *current directory*; this is the directory in which you are working at present. You can change your current directory with the *cd* command, which is described later.

2.2   LISTING A DIRECTORY

Creating files is useless unless you have some way of subsequently examining them — both their names and their contents. The Unix command *ls* lists the contents of your directory; that is, the names of the files therein. If you have created *file1* as described and try using *ls*, you may expect to see the following;

```
$  ls
file1
$
```

If on the other hand you considered the example too trivial to try, and as a new user still have an empty directory, you may expect to see

```
$  ls
$
```

In the first example we are assuming you possess only the one file in your login directory, and *ls* has listed its name. Had you possessed more, *ls* would have listed all their names neatly sorted into alphabetical order. In the second example we are assuming that you have no files, and the response has told you precisely that — no output equals no files. This terseness is a characteristic feature of Unix at work — the system rarely gives you more information than you explicitly ask for. *ls* does not interpret an empty directory as any kind of error, it just has nothing to say.

It is obviously a little heavy handed to have *ls* report on all your files whenever you call it. The command takes **arguments** to make it more selective. If, for instance, we wanted to know whether a file called *file97* was in the current directory, we would say

```
$  ls file97
file97 not found
$
```

In this example, *file97* does not exist. Since we have been specific about what we want to know, *ls* has reported its failure. Had the file existed, we would have seen

```
$  ls file97
file97
$
```

ls has successfully found and reported the presence of *file97*.

2.3   LISTING THE CONTENTS OF A FILE

To list the *contents* of a file, remember *cat* serves to list one file into another one — we can use it to list files in your directory onto the terminal thus

```
$  cat file1
These few words are my first file
$
```

Note the distinction between this use of *cat* and the previous one; here the file name has been given as an argument to *cat* whereas earlier we directed output from *cat* into *file1* by using the direction ">".

This introduces a very deeply rooted Unix principle — unless told otherwise, by, for instance, the use of ">", Unix will assume that you want your input to come from your terminal and your output to go to it. Thus *ls* reported your directory contents *on the terminal*. With no instructions to the contrary, *cat* has interpreted *file1* as an argument, and directed the output of its action, that is, to catenate its argument(s), to the terminal. We shall return to the topic of directing input and output in section 2.7.

cat may take an arbitrary number of arguments; if there are more than one they should be separated by spaces, not commas which could be part of a file name. If you had invested the time in creating five files named *file1*, *file2*, ... *file5* you could list them all by one call to *cat* thus

```
$  cat file1 file2 file3 file4 file5
{The output would appear here}
$
```

The chances are that the output would be confusing, however, since nothing in the output would indicate where *file1* ended and *file2* began, nor where *file2* ended and *file3* began, and so on. *cat* would faithfully list them all, end to end, as asked.

2.4   DELETING, RENAMING, COPYING, ...

You have some files in your directory; it will be a short time before you are going to want to throw them away, or change their names, or perhaps create multiple copies of them. Each of these functions is managed by simple Unix commands.

File *deletion* is accomplished by the *rm* command (an abbreviation of "remove") — thus if you have created *file1* and decide to rid yourself of it, use *rm* thus

```
$  rm file1
$
```

Unix has silently done your bidding. Unless you take special measures, *rm* will not report back after it has performed its deletion. If, however, *file1* did not exist, we would see something like

```
$  rm file1
rm:    file1 nonexistent
$
```

rm has detected something out of the ordinary — it is unable to do as you asked since, as it says, *file1* is nonexistent. Like *cat*, *rm* may take any number of arguments, so if you wanted rid of *file1*, *file2*, ... *file5*, you could use *rm* thus

```
$  rm file1 file2 file3 file4 file5
```

Renaming files introduces the command *mv*, an abbreviation of "move". To rename *file1* we would say

```
$  mv file1 renamed
```

after which whatever was in *file1* would have moved to *renamed*, and *file1* would be no more. Beware, Unix will take you at your word. Should the file *renamed* already exist, *mv* will assume that you know what you are doing and replace it by what was *file1* with no warning.

Similar to *mv* we have the *copy* command *cp* which creates a new copy of a file. We may use it thus

```
$  cp file1 file1again
```

the result of which would be to create a new copy of *file1* called *file1 again*, leaving the original untouched. *cp* will be as unforgiving as *mv* should *file1 again* already exist; it will be thrown away and replaced by a copy of *file1* without warning.

We have met five Unix commands, *cat*, *ls*, *rm*, *mv*, and *cp*, which together should provide a flavour of the Unix vocabulary style; commands may be expected to be highly abbreviated, often to just two letters, but not impossible to decipher. Arguably the action of *cat* is not one you would guess at, but the others are respectably intuitive.

2.5 SOME OTHER ESSENTIALS

We shall look swiftly at five more commands that are useful to have at hand.

Your security measure for most of what you do is your password. Unless another unscrupulous user is looking over your shoulder as you log in, you are secure from unauthorised intruders in your directory. It is clearly a good idea though to be able to change your password from time to time, for which Unix provides the *passwd* command.

```
$  passwd
Changing password for your name
Old password:
```

```
New password:
Retype new password:
$
```

Note the security techniques of not echoing input, ensuring that you meant what you typed by asking for the new password twice, and ensuring that you are who you should be by enquiring the old password first — this should prevent unauthorised users changing your password while you have left your terminal unattended.

Security is enhanced by Unix being reluctant to accept "short" passwords; anything of four or less characters it will consider too short, together with anything of six or less characters that is of one alphabetic case only. *passwd* will only accept such passwords if you persist, but security minded users are advised to take its advice and use at least seven characters.

Most probably you will know other users of the system. You can discover who else is currently logged on by asking *who* of Unix;

```
$  who
brown      tty01   Mar 23   14:45
smith      tty02   Mar 23   17:36
dennis     tty03   Mar 23   19:12
dorothy    tty07   Mar 23   18:57
$
```

You are told who is active on the system, which terminal number they are using and when they logged on.

Something computers are unfailingly good at is telling the time. *date* will get Unix to provide you with the current date and time thus

```
$  date
Wed Mar 23 19:51:07 GMT 1989
```

Note the frills of reporting what day it is and the time zone in addition to the date and time to the second.

Files accumulate quickly; it is easy for your directory to fill with files that look as though they may be copies of one another, or perhaps minor amendments of one another. Unix supplies a swift utility *cmp* that will report whether two files differ, and if so the first occurrence of a difference. Suppose you have three files, *original*, *same* and *alteration* that you suspect are all the same. *cmp* will help you thus;

```
$  cmp original alteration
original alteration differ:    char 68, line 11
$  cmp original same
$
```

We are informed that *alteration* is not the same as *original*, and the
first place at which they differ. We would find that on line eleven something had changed; the change is in fact the sixtyeighth character of the
files (not of the eleventh line of the files). There is no indication of what
the actual difference is, but quite often the mere existence of a difference
is all we need to know. *same* is, however, a copy of *original* — Unix
behaves true to form and says nothing when there is nothing to say. If
we wish to find all the differences between two files, and we are using
a Berkeley Unix system, we could use the *-l* option which provides a
"long" listing. This option is available on some versions of System V,
but not all.

A final command we shall introduce here is *echo*. *echo* will, as its
name implies, echo its argument to you straight away, so you may see

```
$  echo hello
hello
$
```

It may seem at this stage that there can be very little use for such a
parrot and indeed for the novice this is true, and it may be disregarded as
an interesting gadget. *echo* is however a very useful device; as soon as
uses are developed for *scripts*, or any kind of hidden process, the power
to echo will be invaluable; remember its existence.

2.6 HELPING YOURSELF

Many Unix sites offer a useful self-teaching package for the novice and
most provide a mountain of "on-line" documentation that may be called
up at your terminal. To learn the basics, type the command *learn* and you
will be offered a variety of options. *learn* is designed for the beginner and
no further instructions in its use are required here (*learn* is not, regrettably,
available on most versions of Unix System V).

For full documentation, recourse eventually has to be made to the
Unix Programmer's Manual (UPM). This is of course available in hard-

copy book form, but many systems also make it available on-line (although if you are working at a small installation this may not be the case). If a particular command is giving you trouble, or you are curious about its full capabilities, ask for the manual entry on it with the command *man*. We would ask for the entry on *ls* thus

```
$ man ls
```

Often we are not going to know precisely which command we need; some versions of *man* (in particular Berkeley Unix but not Version 7) cater for this eventuality by allowing a *keyword* lookup thus;

```
$ man -k password
getpass (3) - read a password
passwd  (1) - change login password
passwd  (5) - password file
$
```

man has searched the one-line summary of all its entries for the word we gave as a key; it has found three entries that talk about passwords, whose full manual entries we can now call up at will. The mysterious numbers in brackets that appear after the name of the manual page indicate the *section* of the manual in which the information lies. As can be seen in the example above, section 1 is reserved for information about Unix commands, section 3 is reserved for library functions and procedures and section 5 is reserved for information about the format of system files. There are usually eight manual sections; for a full list, the Unix Programmer's Manual should be consulted.

Be warned that the manual aims to provide full documentation and is therefore of necessity rather concise at times. Usually the terminal is not the best place to read several pages of documentation on an extraordinarily fancy command for the first time. That said, the manual is an indispensable and oft-used feature of all Unix systems.

2.7   DIRECTING INPUT AND OUTPUT

We have already said a little about the direction of default input and output. Unix utilities will usually read from *standard input* and write out to *standard output*. By default, both of these are your terminal, which Unix finds indistinguishable from any other kind of file. It is often the case that you would prefer to read from a file in your directory, or write your output into a file, rather than hold a conversation exclusively to and from the screen. The characters ">" and "<", one of which we have already met, provide a powerful mechanism for doing this.

Remember we used the ">" symbol to create a file using *cat*. This is always the action of this symbol when it appears in a command; whatever would have appeared on the screen is deposited instead in a file whose name appears after the symbol. (The shell is not fussy about whether you insert a space before the file name). Thus if you wanted to keep a copy of the current date and time in a file in your directory, you may type

```
$   date >now
$
```

The output of *date* is written into the file called *now* — note that no output appears on your screen, it has all been redirected.

It should not be a surprise to learn that if the file *now* already existed it would be overwritten without warning and its previous contents lost.

Analogous to ">" we have the operator "<" whose action is to redirect standard *input* rather then *output*. The following command

```
$   cat <file1 >file2
```

uses both operators. Remember that without arguments *cat* reads from standard input and writes to standard output. Here we have told it to use *file1* as standard input and *file2* as standard output. The action of the command therefore will be almost exactly the same as

```
$   cp file1 file2
```

That is, take the contents of *file1*, put them in a file and call it *file2*.

In addition to standard input and output, Unix provides a *standard error* output. If a command sends a message to the standard error file it will usually appear on your terminal, and will not be redirected by the > operator. If you wish to redirect standard error you should study either section 5.5 or section 7.5.

Chapter 3

Editing With Ex and Vi

We have seen how to enter text into a file, but we have not established any way to alter that file subsequently. Clearly this will be a necessity in everyday dealings with computers — programs and data that are deposited in files require alteration when mistakes appear, and additions and amendments, major and minor, become necessary as the work develops. All computer systems therefore offer an **editor** of some kind, and generally more than one. Editors come in a variety of shapes and sizes, but their common capability and function is to permit you to examine text selectively, and, more important, to delete, add to and amend text selectively. It is the editor that you will use to correct all your spelling mistakes and omissions.

The number of editors available is effectively uncountable. That said, there is a reasonably well defined subset that is well known, well understood and reliable. The editor that is common to many modern Unix systems is the screen editor *vi*. The *vi* editor was originally released with the Berkeley versions of Unix, but it almost always appears on machines running System V; it is based on the *ed* editor, which is common to *all* Unix systems. Since it is available universally under Unix, *ed* is a lowest common denominator among editors; experienced users are inclined to find it simple. This is a feature which makes it eminently suitable for the novice, but also for use in **shell scripts**. There are many other editors available under Unix; for example, *emacs*, *jove*, *em* and *ned* which you may find supported on your local system. It is often a wise idea to adopt the most popular editor on your local system, if only because more help will be forthcoming if you get stuck! The most common screen-based editor that is currently available under Unix is *vi*; since it provides a command set which includes the *ed* command set, we will use it in this chapter. Fluency in *vi* will provide a good springboard for learning other Unix editors.

Once you have a grasp of *vi*, you may find it easier to edit referring to Appendix C, which contains a summary of commands.

26

3.1   GETTING STARTED WITH *ex*

It is important to understand from the very beginning that *vi* is two editors
under one name — a screen editor, called *vi*, and a line editor, called *ex*.
Although *vi* is designed to run on visual display terminals that are capable
of various clever operations (such as cursor addressing), you can use *ex*
on any kind of terminal at all. Since *ex* is the "basic" mode of *vi*, and is
similar to *ed*, we will discuss it first. The simplest way to summon *ex* is
to call it by name thus

```
$   ex
```

You should see the response

```
$   ex
:
```

The ":" prompt is *ex* saying "ready for a command"; you are now
ready to edit an existing file or to create a new one. Assuming that you
are starting from scratch, the most likely command we would use here
is *a*, standing for *append*, meaning that we want to append some text.
Many commands are single letters like this, standing for editing verbs.

You may justifiably ask what the editor proposes to append to; in
common with most other text editors, *ex* operates in a *buffer*. Although its
job is to amend files, it will not tamper with existing files until explicitly
told so to do. Instead the work in hand, in this case our *append*, is done
in a scratch work area called the buffer. We may add text to, delete text
from and make amendments to the text within the buffer at will, and only
when we are satisfied with it will it be committed to a file.

Suppose we have entered the *a* command as suggested.

```
$   ex
:a
```

Notice that *ex* offers very little response — it simply fails to print a
":" prompt. You should be growing used to this behaviour by now from
Unix utilities — in the absence of an error message we may assume that
the editor is now waiting for us to give it some text that it can append to
its (empty) buffer. Whatever is now typed goes verbatim into the buffer,

and will do so until the editor sees you type the ⓒcharacter or a line containing only a full-stop.[1] This is the signal to *ed* that you have completed the text you wish to enter. If the purpose of the editing session were to write a program, we would just type in the program; if it were to create a file of data we would type in the data just as we wanted it to appear.

```
$ex
:a
a
very
short
file
.
:
```

Presuming that the input text contains no mistakes, it will now be ready for depositing into a file. Use the *w*, standing for *write*, command to do this. *w* takes a single argument, the name of the file you want to write into. After it has done this *ex* should respond with a message such as:

```
:w simplefile
"simplefile" [New file] 4 lines, 18 characters
:
```

indicating that the file is a new one, and it contains 4 lines of text with 18 characters. If it responds with

```
:w simplefile
"simplefile" File exists -
         use "w!  simplefile" to overwrite
:
```

then the file called *simplefile* already exists. The message from *vi* indicates that you can overwrite the existing copy of *simplefile* by using the *w!* command instead of the *w* command; at this stage, try choosing a different name for your file.

The third, very simple command that you will need early on is *q*, standing for *quit*, which will terminate the editing session and return you to the shell. A very simple editing session may then look like this:

---

[1]This is not quite true; entering the interrupt character will stop the editor behaving properly.

```
$  ex
:a
a
very
short
file
.
:w simplefile
"simplefile" [New file] 4 lines, 18 characters
:q
$
```

after which the file *simplefile* will contain the eighteen characters given
(comprising the fourteen visible characters in the four words, together
with four *newline* characters, one at the end of each line).

The error messages from *ex* are slightly more informative than the
messages from its predecessor, *ed*. If you attempt to quit from *ex* without
writing out the buffer, you will get the message

```
:q
No write since last change (:quit!  overrides)
:
```

whereas *ed* would simply give you the message "?". If you are determined to quit without writing the buffer, simply type the command *q!*.

Essential Editor Commands

So far we have done nothing with *ex* that we have not seen done with *cat*;
we have merely created a file typed at the terminal. Let us now suppose
that we have a file to which we wish to make some changes. In this case,
we will tell the editor as we summon it what the name of the file is by
providing the filename as an argument on the command line; hence, if
we wish to amend *simplefile* we would type

```
$  ex simplefile
"simplefile" 4 lines, 18 characters
:
```

The message from *ex* confirms the file name, and indicates the size
of the file. If the file is non-existent or cannot be found, you will get the
message

```
$ ex newfile
"newfile" [New file]
:
```

Otherwise you may be confident that a *copy of* the chosen file now resides in the buffer waiting for your attention.

Like most editors, *ex* has a concept of *current position* within the file — you may think of this as a pointer placed at some position in your text. This pointer is placed conceptually at the beginning of a line; the pointer refers to a line address, of which the simplest form is a line number (*ex* is thus a *line-oriented* editor). Immediately after you enter the editor it has scanned the whole file so that it can report the number of characters and lines; for this reason, the pointer is positioned on the last line of the file when you enter your first command.

Moving the pointer is simply a matter of giving the line number that you wish to move to. Thus, typing *1* will send it to line one, and typing *4000* will send it to line four thousand (if it exists). If the line doesn't exist, *ex* simply says "Not that many lines in buffer"; if the line does exist, *ex* will print out the line by way of confirmation. This system only works if you have a good idea of the precise number of lines in your file and where the interesting areas are located; an impractical demand for any except the smallest files. For this reason *ex* makes available the symbol "$" (dollar) which always refers to the *last* line, and "." (dot) which refers to the *current* line. In addition, we can move relative to the current position by using +*n* and −*n* which move the pointer forward and backward *n* lines respectively from dot. Thus, −2 will move the pointer back 2 lines. These ideas should become clearer as you begin to use them in practice.

Most probably, the first action you require is to see a section of the file; the *ex* command required is *p* (for *print*). On its own *p* will print out the current line. More usefully you can precede it with two line numbers separated by a comma, and *ex* will display all the lines between those numbers. Thus, *1,$p* prints out the entire file;

```
$ ex simplefile
"simplefile" 4 lines, 18 characters
:1,$p
a
very
short
```

```
file
:
```

A (possibly confusing) action of *p* is to move the pointer as it prints, so after the command is obeyed the pointer is at the second of the two line numbers given. Notice incidentally that *6,3p* will elicit a complaint from *ex* — it is observing that the first number is larger than the second.

Searching, and Line Numbers By Context

It is quite probable that you are not going to know the precise line numbers of the areas of text that you wish to examine; in this case you can set your location by *searching* for the text you want to look at. We search for a string by typing a "/" followed by the string in which we are interested, followed by another "/". Thus, if we know a file contains the string "somewhere in the" we can type

```
:/somewhere in the/
... this string is somewhere in the file ...
:
```

The action of the command is to move the pointer forward from the current position to the first line containing the requested string, and then to type it out. "Forward" in this sense interprets line one as following line "$", so the buffer is considered to be circular. Should the string that you have requested not exist, *ex* will complain as you may expect; the response will be "**Pattern not found**" and the pointer will not move.

The action of setting the pointer to the the number of the searched-out line makes the search command a powerful tool to combine with other commands. If, for instance, we are ignorant of the line numbers in a particular file but we wish to print out all lines between those containing the words "beginning" and "end" we may type

```
:/beginning/, /end/p
```

The individual search commands are interchangeable with line numbers — we may use this feature with all commands that take line number arguments.

A useful feature of the search command is its memory; typing

```
://
```

will execute a search for the last looked-for string, starting from the current position. This is especially useful for searching for occurrences of an oft-repeated string.

A word of warning at this point — ambitious users will find the *search* and related commands behaving oddly for strings that include any of the following characters;

```
. * ~ & ( ) [ ] ^ $ \
```

These are the so called *metacharacters* described more fully later in this chapter.

Amending Text

A principal purpose of editing is to correct mistakes, for which the *s* (*substitute*) command is used. Suppose we have arrived at the line

```
this line contains a speling mistake
```

We use the *s* command to specify the string we wish to change, and then the string we wish to change it to, the strings being delimited by the "/" character; in this case we may type

```
:s/speling/spelling/
:p
this line contains a spelling mistake
:
```

Remember that the pointer is considered to be at the beginning of the line, so we need to exercise care in specifying the correct string — for example

```
:s/li/lli/
:p
this lline contains a speling mistake
```

The substitution is performed on the *first* occurrence of the string in the line. Should we be positioned on the wrong line, *s* can take a line number argument.

Justifiably you might observe that entering line after line of commands always followed by a *p* to check the result will become very tedious. *ex* will allow limited construction of composite commands to accelerate matters. Thus

```
:1001s/peli/pelli/p
```

would take us to line 1001, perform a substitution of "pelli" for "peli" and then print out the result. If we did not know exactly which line the error was on, we could type

```
:/speling/s/peli/pelli/p
```

and use the search as a line number argument. *p* may follow most commands in this fashion to provide verification of current position.

In fact, *s*, like *p*, can take two line arguments. Issuing the command

```
:1,100s/speling/spelling/
```

will correct the first occurrence of our mistake on each line between one and one hundred inclusive, and

```
:1,$s/speling/spelling/
```

will do the same on each line of the file — a useful and common command.

Text Deletion

Should a line require complete deletion, use the *d* command. *d* alone will delete the current line, and like *s* and *p*, will accept one or two line numbers as arguments; for example

```
:5,10d
```

deletes lines five to ten inclusive.

Text Insertion

Should new blocks of text require inserting, use either the *a* command, which we have already met, or the *i* (for *insert*) command. Their action is very similar; once issued, all typed text is written verbatim into the buffer until the appearance of a line containing a single full stop. *a* will put the new text *after* the current line, and *i* will place it before. Both of these may take a single argument to specify a line number, so there is no need to position yourself accurately before issuing the command. Since *ex* allows you to use the command *0a* to insert before line 1, you do not strictly need both commands; however, you will certainly find each command convenient at different times.

Block Alteration

Another useful way to enter blocks of text is with *c*, the *change* command. All text following this command is put into the buffer just as with the *a* and *i* commands, except that its action is to overwrite the current (or specified lines). Thus, if we wanted to rewrite completely lines one to five we would type

```
:1,5c
```

Notice *c* would allow such a replacement to include as many or as few lines as we please.

If we wanted to *move* text rather than overwrite, we use the *m* command. This will pick up a block of text, specified by two line numbers in the usual way, and deposit it after a third specified line number, given after the *m*. Thus to move lines one to five to the end of the file we might say

```
:1,5m$
```

Remember that line numbers may always be specified by search commands; large block transfers of text are thus made possible with no knowledge of their precise position in the file. For example, if a file contains blocks of text thus;

This block of text
    { in here is an arbitrary number of lines }

    needs moving.
       { more text }
    The block requires placing after HERE.

then we may move the block in which we are interested thus:

```
:/This block of text/, /needs moving/m/after HERE/
```

Undoing Mistakes While Editing

It will be a common event for you to have edited something in error — if you have just executed a complicated substitution on a line and you did not mean it, it could be an unpleasant task to have to undo it. Fortunately, most versions of *ex* provide *undo* for you with the *u* command. Typing *u* will return matters to their state preceding your last command (provided you have not changed line since issuing it).

Reading/Writing Files

Quite frequently you will want to change files during an editing session, perhaps to read in a new file, or to begin editing a different file, or to write out an intermediate state of your editing. We have already met the *w* command that writes files out to a specified name. If we have entered the editor by

```
$  ex filename
```

then *w* will assume that we wish to rewrite the file to *filename* if we give it no argument. This is usually the case and provides a useful shorthand. If we wish to change this default filename, the command *f* will do it for us thus;

```
:f newfilename
```

    Following this, all subsequent *w* commands (without arguments) will write to *newfilename*.
    Frequently it is useful to be able to read in another complete file and add it to the one we are editing. The

```
:r filename
```

command achieves this, placing the text of the file after the current position. If we wished to add the new text to the end of the buffer, the
command

```
:$r filename
```

would do this. After *r* is executed, the pointer is set at the end of the
inserted text.

Another way of calling a new file into the buffer is with the *e* (for
edit) command, which takes a filename as argument. This will *overwrite*
the buffer with the named file, discarding its original contents, so if they
are wanted the command should be preceded by *w*. The usual use of *e* is
to start editing a new file without bothering to return to the Unix prompt;
thus an editing session may look like;

```
$ ex file1
{do some editing, and write out the results}
:w
:e file2
{do some more on file2}
:w
:e file3
{and so on}
```

Note that the *e* command usefully resets the default filename written
to by the *w* command.

Global Commands

The commands we have met so far nearly all respond to line number
arguments; various ways of circumventing the problem of not knowing
precise line numbers have been provided. We do not, however, have a
satisfactory way of executing an editor command throughout the file. For
instance, if we have misspelled a commonly used word we shall need to
make a *global* replacement of the misspelling. We use the *g* command to
do this. *g* is followed by a search string and some normal *ed* commands.
The commands are then executed on all lines in the file that contain the
search string; for example

```
:g/speling/s//spelling/p
```

locates all lines containing the string "speling" and converts the first occurrence on that line to "spelling", printing out the result afterwards. Notice that the first argument to the *s* command has been left empty — this is a shorthand way of saying "use the global search string here". In addition,

```
:g/speling/s//spelling/g
```

will correct *all* occurrences of the error, catching multiple appearances on one line.

To cater for all tastes, an "inverse" to the *g* command is available.

```
:v/string/{commands}
```

will execute the given commands on all lines that do *not* contain the specified string; for example

```
:v/speling/d
```

would delete all lines in the file that did not contain our misspelling.

Further Commands

Many users discover that an understanding of the commands we have met so far is sufficient for all their editing. Now you are able to search for, amend, delete and insert text you can do all that the editor is designed to do. *ex*, however, can be a sophisticated tool for the more experienced user. The remainder of this chapter could well be skipped on a first reading but when you feel you have a sound understanding of what has gone before you can graduate to "expert" user by reading on. What follows (and indeed, what has gone before) is not intended to be an exhaustive *ex* manual. Having mastered the contents of this chapter, reference to the Unix *ex* manual will complete your education.

Metacharacters

So far when we have been specifying a string we have demanded that
it be entered explicitly. Frequently this is going to be clumsy, tedious
or, indeed, not precisely what we want. Often we will want to focus on
the occurrence of a string at, say, the beginning or end of the line. *ex*
provides a number of *metacharacters* to answer this and other needs. A
metacharacter is any character that has some special meaning — they
need to be used with care since they are not interpreted literally.

Line beginning and line end are denoted by the characters ˆ and *$*
respectively. Their use is quite simple;

```
:/ˆstring/
```

will seek out the next occurrence of "string" at the beginning of a line,
and

```
:/string$/
```

will similarly find it at the end of a line. The symbols may be combined,
so

```
:/ˆstring$/
```

will find a line containing just the word "string".

Equally useful is the *wildcard* feature "." which will match any single
character. If, for example, we wish to find an occurrence of two *p*'s
separated by one other character (we care not which), we would type

```
:/p.p/
```

Of course, if we are looking for a word at the end of a sentence we
are now in trouble, since

```
:/string./
```

will not (necessarily) settle on the occurrence of "string" preceding a
full stop, but on the next occurrence of "string" preceding *any* character
(i.e. probably the next occurrence of "string"). We need some way of
interpreting full stop, and other metacharacters, literally, and we do this

by the device of *escaping* them, meaning that they are preceded by a special character sequence that informs *ex* that they are to be interpreted literally. The sequence used is a single character, the backslash "\" (many Unix commands and programs use the idea of an *escape character*, and you may always expect it to be done with the backslash character). The example above should thus be written

```
:/string\ ./
```

Likewise, had we wanted to find an occurrence of "string$" we would type

```
:/string\ $/
```

and if we had wanted this string at the end of a line, we would type

```
:/string\ $$/
```

Here the first dollar is interpreted literally while the second is interpreted as "end of line".

The backslash translates any metacharacter, in particular itself — thus

```
:/\\/
```

locates the next occurrence of a single backslash.

Very often strings we wish to locate contain an unknown number of repeated characters. We may wish to find a line like

```
    left          right
```

where the two words are separated by some spaces. We can save the trouble of explicit counting by using the "*" character, which is interpreted as "multiple". It follows some character that we would like repeated; thus

```
:/left *right/
```

locates the two words "left" and "right" separated by any number, *including zero*, of spaces, while

```
:/left.*right/
```

will find the two words separated on one line by *any* set of characters.

It is remarkably useful to be able to specify sets of characters, although constructs like ".*" are often too wide ranging, since they will match any sequence of characters at all. We can define a set of characters by enclosing them in square brackets; thus if we are looking for a single digit we may type

```
:/[0123456789]/
```

and the editor will match any one of the characters inside the brackets. Of course, if we are looking for a *stream* of digits we may now type

```
:/[0123456789]*/
```

and the asterisk will take care of the repetition as noted above. A useful shorthand supported here is that we may type "0-9" to indicate "any digit", and "A-Z" or "a-z" to indicate upper or lower case letters respectively — *ex* knows the sensible order for characters.

A final metacharacter is "&". It has a simple, convenient definition when used as part of the replacement string of a substitution; it simply copies the string to be replaced. It is used to save retyping long or complicated expressions to be matched; thus

```
:s/tedious expression/(&)/
```

would parenthesise the first instance of *tedious expression* .

Advanced Substitution

Advanced use of *s* is now straightforward. Remember that all that is required is a string to be replaced and the proposed replacement. We are at liberty to use any of the metacharacters in specifying what we want to change, so for example

```
:g/[0-9][0-9]*/s//NUMBER/g
```

will replace all digit streams on each line with the string *NUMBER*. Notice we have to specify the string carefully; globally searching for *[0-9]** would have matched digit streams of length zero in addition to the ones we were actually searching for, which might have curious results.

We now also have a swift way of adding text at line beginnings and ends — for instance we may append text to a line end by

```
:s/$/this text added/
```

We are replacing "line end" by some text.

A not unreasonable question is, what happens if we have a line like:

```
left left left ... some text ... right right right
```

and we issue the following substitution command?

```
:s/left.*right/hello/
:p
```

When *ex* matches metacharacters, it always attempts to find the *longest* match possible — as a result, the last example would actually produce:

```
:s/left.*right/hello/
:p
hello
```

Executing Unix Commands Within *ex*

You are bound to discover sooner or later that, in the middle of an edit, you need some information from Unix. It may be just the time of day, but more plausibly you may want a directory listing to check on the existence or otherwise of some particular file. Fortunately, Unix and *ex* permit this — if you type *!* (an exclamation mark) followed by *any* Unix command, your editing state will be suspended and the command executed. All output of the command appears on the screen as usual, after which another *!* is printed and your editing session continues. An example may be;

```
$ ex FILE
"FILE" 4 lines, 18 characters
:!ls
FILE
insert.1
insert.2
!
:r insert.1
```

Before appending *insert.1* to the *ed* buffer, *ls* has been used to check on the file names. The second "!" character, output by *ed*, indicates that the incidental output is complete, and the editor has regained control.

If you are using a version of Berkeley Unix, you will probably find it easier to make use of *job control.* For a brief description, you should study section 7.8 in Chapter 7.

A particularly useful feature is being able to edit other files from within *ex.* There is no restriction on the command you may issue.

3.2   GETTING STARTED WITH *vi*

We have now covered almost all of the important details about the *ex* editor; if you have worked your way through the material above it should be relatively easy for you to use an editor such as *ed. ed* is very similar to *ex*, except that it is much less verbose — it only has two error messages, "?" and "??". However, it is ideal for incorporating editing tasks into files of shell commands, so it remains common to all Unix systems.

If you have a visual display terminal, you can probably use the *screen-editing* side of *ex*, called *vi. ex* and *vi* are simply different faces of the same editor; *vi* provides a much more "interactive" mode of editing than *ex.* To start *vi*, simply type

```
$ vi
```

If *vi* is capable of driving your terminal there will be a short pause, after which your screen will go blank; the cursor which marks the *current position* in the text should now be in the top left-hand corner, and the left hand side of the screen should be a column of """ characters. The """ character is *vi*'s way of saying that the line on the screen is past the end of the text. As you explore *vi* you may see lines with a "@" sign on them; these indicate that the line has been deleted, but *vi* has not yet fully updated the display.

Warning: when you begin to learn *vi* it is very easy to get lost, since there is very little response from *vi* to tell you what *mode* you are in; *vi* has two basic modes — *Command Mode* and *Insert Mode*. When you are in command mode, *vi* is ready to accept a command to edit the file or to move around it; when you are in text entry mode, almost everything you type goes into your file as text and appears on the screen as you type it.

Special Characters

Have a look at your keyboard — there should be a key marked with the characters "ESC" or "ESCAPE" — if not, you can use the control and "[" keys to produce the same character. The ESCAPE key should always return you to command mode in *vi*, from whence you can issue other commands or quit. If you're not sure what state you are in at any time, you can usually recover by hitting ESCAPE a few times. If you are in command mode, pressing ESCAPE will cause *vi* to produce an audible or visible beep (that is, the terminal bell will ring or the screen will blink); this lets you know that you're in command mode. The RETURN key is used to terminate commands in *ex* mode. The INTERRUPT key, ⓵, is a forceful way of getting back to command mode; if *vi* appears to be beyond recall, try pressing ⓵.

Switching Between *ex* and *vi*

While you are in *vi*, you can escape temporarily into *ex* to issue an *ex* command — for instance, you can issue global substitute commands or file read/write commands from *ex* mode. To get into *ex* mode from *vi* command mode, type a ":" key. You should see a ":" appear on the bottom line of your screen, at the left-hand side:

```
top of screen
~
~
~
~
~
:
```

You can now enter an *ex* command — not forgetting to end it with the RETURN key. When you finish an *ex* command, you will jump back into *vi* command mode.

Getting Out of *vi*

To quit from *vi* you must be in command mode. The simplest way out is the *quit* command from *ex* — enter the sequence *:q* to go to *ex* mode and enter the *quit* command. If you have edited your file in any way, you will probably want to save it; to do this, use the *write* command from *ex* — enter the sequence *:w*. As with *ex*, you can write to a new file by using the sequence

```
~

~

~

:w newfile
```

vi will respond with a message indicating the size of the file, and then return you to *vi* command mode. Note that *vi* uses the bottom line of the screen as a *command line* — *ex* commands are entered on this line, and responses appear on the same line. After writing your file you can then quit in the usual manner. Quite often, you will want to write your file and then quit immediately; you can do this using the *x*, standing for *exit,* command. Typing ":x" will write your file and then exit from *vi*. If you want to write to a different file, you can enter

```
~

~

~

:x newfile
```

Entering Text

Table 3.1 lists the basic *vi* commands for inserting text. Notice that the *a* and *i* commands append and insert text from the current position in the file, whereas *o* and *O* will *open* lines for new text. For example, let us assume that you want to insert the text "Hello there"; if we assume that the current position is the position marked by ☐, and use the initial text:

Vi Insert Commands	
Character	**Function**
a	append from current position
i	insert before current position
o	open line below
O	open line above

Table 3.1: Insertion Commands

```
This is a line of text
And this is another line
And this is what I want to say.. .
~
~
```

(which would make the last "." in the line the current position) then we would get the following results: firstly, using *a*,

```
This is a line of text
And this is another line
And this is what I want to say...Hello ther e
~
~
```

Secondly, using *i*,

```
This is a line of text
And this is another line
And this is what I want to say..Hello ther e .
~
~
```

Thirdly, using *o*,

```
This is a line of text
And this is another line
And this is what I want to say...
Hello ther e
~
~
```

Insert-Mode Editing Characters	
Character	**Function**
^h	erase last character
ⓒ	erase last character
^w	erase last word

Table 3.2: Insert-Mode Editing Characters

And lastly, using *O*,

```
This is a line of text
And this is another line
Hello ther e
And this is what I want to say...
~
~
```

Bear in mind that you must use the ESCAPE character to get out of insert mode and back into command mode.

While you are in insert mode you can use a number of editing characters, as described in table 3.2. *vi* provides a number of additional commands to insert text, but first we discuss ...

Moving Around Your File

vi provides a wide variety of commands to allow you to move the current position around your file. Some commands are very simple — they allow you to move a character, a word, a line or a page at a time. *vi* also "understands", to a limited extent, what constitutes a sentence and a paragraph, and provides movement commands that apply to them.

Let's look at the basic movement commands in table 3.3 to begin with; these can be split into groups, for character and line positioning. Remember that these are *commands*, so they must be entered while *vi* is in command mode. On most keyboards, the *arrow keys* will also work as expected. Notice that the line positioning commands come in two flavours — the *j* and *k* commands will always remember the current column as you move up and down through the file — the current position

Character Positioning Commands	
Character	**Function**
h	forward one character
space	forward one character
l	backward one character
^h	backward one character
$	forward to end-of-line
^	backward to beginning-of-line
Line Positioning Commands	
j	next line, same column
+	next line, at first non-white
k	previous line, same column
−	previous line, at first non-white
G	go to a line (last line by default)

Table 3.3: Positioning Commands

will stay the same distance from the left-hand margin (as much as possible); the − and + commands will look for the first non-blank character on the line.

vi also provides commands to allow you to move by words and sentences — see table 3.4. *vi* also allows you to prefix a positioning command with a count. For example, suppose we had the following display:

```
Here is some simple text
Here is a nother line of simple text
~
~
~
```

with the current position on the first letter of "another". A single *w* command would move the current position as follows:

```
Here is some simple text
Here is another line of simple text
~
```

Word and Sentence Positioning Commands	
Character	**Function**
w	move forward a word
b	move backward a word
e	move forward to end-of-word
)	move forward a sentence
(	move backward a sentence

Table 3.4: Word and Sentence Positioning Commands

We can prefix a *w* command with a count to move a number of words; bear in mind that we do this in command mode — the count will **not** appear on the screen. Suppose we type *3w* — the result would be

```
Here is some simple text
Here is another line of simple t ext
-
```

We can move backwards using the *b* command, so typing *4b* would result in

```
Here is some simple text
Here is a nother line of simple text
-
```

which is logical enough, since that's where we started from. All of the the positioning commands in the table above can be prefixed with a count.

vi also provides the *G* (standing for *go*) command. By itself, the *G* command will move the current position onto the last line of the text, but you can prefix the *G* command with a line number. So, for instance, you could enter *42G* to position yourself on line 42. Since this is a positioning *command*, it must be entered while you are in command mode.

Searching

vi also allows you to move the current position in your text by *searching*, in much the same way as *ex*. From *vi* command mode, you can type one of the search characters "/" (for "search forwards") and "?" (for "search backwards"). Typing one of these characters leaves you on the last line of the screen, with *vi* waiting for you to enter a search string. *vi* understands the same search strings (and the same metacharacters) as *ex*, so you can enter search strings like:

```
~
~
~
:/left.*right/
```

The search string is terminated with a RETURN. *vi* will search for the next occurrence of the string and put the current position at the beginning of the string. The previous search string could produce a final display like this:

```
and while we're on the subject, what is the
difference between left and right in the
quantum world?
```

If the string cannot be found *vi* will warn you and leave the current position untouched. Like *ex*, *vi* allows you to add an offset to a search string - a search pattern such as:

```
~
~
:/left.*right/+1
```

will move the current position to the line *after* the matching line. In the same way,

```
~
~
:?left.*right?+1
```

will search backwards for a matching line and place the current position on the following line.

Combining Movement with Operators

One of the most powerful and useful features of *vi* is the facility to combine a **positioning command** with an **editing command** — *vi* allows you to say things like "delete the next three words", for example. In order to do this, *vi* provides a set of editing *operators* which can be applied to sections of your text — you can specify the section by using the movement commands.

The basic grammar of these combined commands is always the same — first you specify the operator and then you specify the positioning command. The positioning command provides a *target* for the operator.

For example, *vi* provides the *d* operator (standing for *delete*). If you wanted to delete the word following the current position, you would type a *d* (for "delete") followed by *w* (for "move forward one word"). So, typing *dw* would change:

```
Here is some simple text
Here is  a nother line of simple text
~
~
```

into

```
Here is some simple text
Here is  l ine of simple text
~
~
```

In the same way, typing *db* would change:

```
Here is some simple text
Here is  a nother line of simple text
~
~
```

into:

```
Here is some simple text
Here  a nother line of simple text
~
~
```

Vi Operators	
Character	**Function**
d	delete
c	change
y	yank

Table 3.5: *Vi* Operators

You can apply the *d* operator to all of the positioning commands that you have seen so far. So, *d*space will delete the character at the current position and *d3w* will delete the three words following the current position.

If you use the *d* operator with the line positioning commands in table 3.3, you may be surprised by the result. The reason is quite simple — when you issue a command such as *d3w*, *vi* takes the following course of actions:

1. mark the current position

2. execute the positioning command

3. apply the operator to the text between the mark and the current position

In the case of commands like *dj*, the mark will be placed on the current line and the new position will be on the next line — the *d* operator will then apply between the two, deleting **both** lines. Not quite what you expected? Well, it can be surprising the first time it happens to you.

The common *vi* operators are listed in table 3.5. These operators can be combined with any of the move commands to produce a wide variety of editing operations. Ignoring *yank* for the moment, a list of examples is given in table 3.6. All of these operators have "short-hand" forms for applying to lines — the commands *dd* and *cc* will delete and change the current line. Like most editing commands, these "short-hand" forms can take a numeric prefix, so you can type *3dd* to delete the next three lines or *3cc* to change the next three lines.

Combined Command Results	
Command	**Result**
dw	delete current word
db	delete previous word
d$	delete to end-of-line
d^	delete to beginning-of-line
d/left.*right/	search for the next occurence of the search string and delete from the current line to the matching line
cw*text*ESC	change next word — *vi* will enter insert mode while the new text is entered. To return to command mode, use ESCAPE.
c$*text*ESC	change to end-of-line — *vi* will enter insert mode while new text is entered. To return to command mode, use ESCAPE.

Table 3.6: Combined Commands

Yanking and Putting

Like most editors, *vi* allows you to copy and move sections of text from
one part of your file to another; in *vi* the mechanism is called *yanking* and
putting. "Yanking" allows you to take a section of text out of your file and
put it into a temporary *yank buffer*; you can then move to a new position
in the file and drop the text back in the file again by "putting". The
simplest form of the *y* command is the "short-hand" form for applying to
the current line — if you have a text section like this:

```
Text line 1
Text |l|ine 2
Text line 3
~
~
```

with the current position on line 2, typing *yy* will yank line 2 into the
yank buffer. You can now use the *p* (for *put*) command to put the yank
buffer back into the file, producing:

```
Text line 1
Text line 2
|T|ext line 2
Text line 3
~
~
```

Notice that the current position moves to the beginning of the line of
text that you have inserted. This technique can be applied to any section
of text; for example, typing *y3w* would yank the three words following
the current position. Typing *p* will now insert them *after the current
position*. So, typing *y3w* and then *p* will convert:

```
Text line 1
|T|ext line 2
Text line 3
~
~
```

into:

```
Text line 1
 T Text line 2ext line 2
Text line 3
 ~
 ~
```

which may not be what you want. The alternative form of the *put* command, which insert text *before* the current position, is *P*. So, typing *y3w* and then *P* will convert:

```
Text line 1
 T ext line 2
Text line 3
 ~
 ~
```

into:

```
Text line 1
Text line 2 Text line 2
Text line 3
 ~
 ~
```

Some examples of yank-and-put sequences are given in table 3.7; as you begin to see, the facility to combine operators with positioning commands allows you to construct extremely powerful commands with very few keystrokes.

Adjusting the Screen

As you use *vi*, you may find that the area of text that the screen allows you to see is wrong — you may want the line with current position on it to be at the top of the screen or at the bottom of the screen. (You may not want it on the screen at all, but that can make editing rather difficult.) Alternatively, one of your colleagues may have sent a message to your terminal which has messed up *vi*'s display. *vi* provides a set of commands that allow you to adjust or refresh your screen. The simplest of these is ^L, which will re-draw the display and tidy it up; unfortunately, some terminals use ^L for cursor motion, which will prevent this refresh

Yank and Put Commands	
Command	**Result**
yyp	yank the current line into the yank buffer and insert it *after* the current position
yyP	yank the current line into the yank buffer and insert it *before* the current position
3yyP	yank the three lines following the current position into the yank buffer then insert them *before* the current position
y10Gp	yank everything between the current position and line 10 into the yank buffer then insert it *before* the current position

Table 3.7: Yank and Put Commands

Vi z Commands	
Command	**Result**
z.	redraw, current position at centre
z–	...at bottom
zCR	...at top

Table 3.8: *Vi z* Commands

command from being used. The ^R command is like ^L, but it will also remove "@" lines (if you have any). The *z* commands allow you to adjust the current position on the screen — see table 3.8. Sometimes, you want to scroll the text up or down a few lines, rather than using the ^F or ^B commands. The ^Y and ^E commands will scroll the text up or down by 1 line at a time. As with so many *vi* commands, you can prefix these commands with a number — typing *5^Y* will scroll up by five lines.

3.3   FURTHER READING

It should be emphasised that this chapter is not an exhaustive *vi* manual, although it is respectably comprehensive and does cover all of the major features of the editor. Reference to Appendix C will give you a reference card of the commands; reference to the Unix manual will tell you even the things you don't want to know.

Chapter 4

Files, Directories and Users

We have spoken a little about the concept of *directory*. Your terminal session commences in your *login* or *home directory*, which is (usually) a different directory for each user, thus permitting different users to create different files which may have the same name — the fact that they lie in different directories saves any ambiguity. These separate directories are not, though, completely divorced from one another, but lie on a *tree* that includes as its *nodes* all the directories and files of the system. This tree has a *root* which may be regarded as the parent of all other directories — it is called /. The Unix system is partitioned into various component parts that live in directories directly below this "root", usually consisting of;

bin programs that implement system commands

dev files which represent devices

etc other "system" programs and files

lib various library programs

tmp a temporary, scratch area

usr files and directories pertaining to users

These definitions are necessarily, at this stage, rather imprecise, but it can be seen that a user's directories, and in particular her login directory, may be expected to lie in the *usr* category. On some systems login directories lie at the next "level" of the tree — on others there may be a further partitioning of the users before arriving at the true "user" level. On some recent versions of Unix (including System VR4 and SUNOS 4), this directory tree has been quite radically redesigned; home directories are held under the directory /*home*, files that are intended to be shared by many machines in a network are held in /*share* and files that are local to a particular machine (log files and spool files in particular) are held in /*var*.

Exactly what the directory structure at your installation is can be determined by using the *pwd*, (print working directory) command. *pwd* will
reply with the *full* name of the directory you are currently in, thus;

```
$   pwd
/usr/yourname
$
```

tells you that you are in a directory directly below *usr*. The "*/*" appearing
between *yourname* and *usr* tells you that *usr* is itself a directory; the
slash indicates one step down the tree away from the root. *pwd* may
alternatively report

```
$   pwd
/usr/yourgroup/yourname
```

indicating that there is another level of tree, called *yourgroup*, lying between your login directory and the root; it is possible that there will be
more such levels than this, but whatever the total number each one will
be revealed by a slash in the reply given by *pwd*.

We can draw a diagram to denote this — see Figure 4.1. In the directories at the bottom of the tree lie the files that we create, delete and

Figure 4.1: The Structure of the Directory Tree

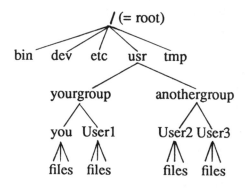

manipulate. If we wish to be quite unambiguous about naming a particular file, we will specify the whole directory tree above it; thus if *FILE*

exists in your directory, which is part of the shown structure, this would be
/usr/yourgroup/yourname/FILE; this full specification is called the *pathname* of *FILE*.

Knowledge of the tree structure can be exploited by the "Change
Directory" command *cd* which allows us to alter current directory; if, for
instance, *User1* owns some files of interest it will be convenient to site
ourselves in her directory thus;

```
$   cd /usr/yourgroup/User1
```

and now all reference we make to files will default to *User1*'s directory.
ls for example, will list all files in the directory */usr/yourgroup/User1*.

Clearly it will be tedious to explicitly enter the */usr/* ... sequence each
time a directory change is required. Unix provides a very useful short-
hand to save this; the directory " .. " (two dots) always refers to the directory above the *current* one in the tree — it is usually called the *parent*
directory. Thus if the diagram represents the directory structure of your
system and you type

```
$   cd ..
```

directly after logging in, you move to */usr/yourgroup*. Repeating the command moves you to */usr* and repeating it a third time moves you to the
root, */*. Since the root is the "end" of the tree it is no longer meaningful
to attempt the command again — it can be tried although it has no effect;
you will remain in directory */*.

In a similar way, the current directory — that provided by *pwd* —
may be abbreviated to " . " (dot).

Issuing the *cd* command without any arguments will return you to
your login directory; it is often useful after a lengthy session of moving
from directory to directory to be able to say

```
$   cd
```

and be sure of the directory to which you are moving.

4.1   SUBDIRECTORIES

A very powerful feature of Unix is its facility for allowing you to extend
the tree *downwards*. You are at liberty to construct *subdirectories* of your
own to an arbitrary depth. This feature is of the greatest use for organising
and keeping track of files, and since the creation of the subtree is in the
power of individual users, each can impose her own cataloguing system,
pertinent to her own collection of files.

Subdirectories are created with the *mkdir* (make directory) command.
The command is followed by the name of the directory to be created, thus;

```
$  mkdir subdir
```

Always provided you had the requisite permission, the subdirectory
subdir will now have been appended to the bottom of the tree at the point
at which the command was issued; if this point is your login directory, the
directory */usr/yourgroup/yourname/subdir* will now exist, and using *cd* it
will be possible to move into it. Moving down the tree with *cd* requires
only the name of the next directory down since the command thinks from
"current position"; thus

```
$  cd subdir
```

will move to the newly created subdirectory.

Observe that the command *ls*, issued directly after *subdir* was created
would have revealed a file called "subdir" in its parent directory. Unix
finds files and directories almost indistinguishable — a directory is just a
file that is a home for other files.

Remembering that *ls* takes arguments, it should now be clear that

```
$  ls /usr/anothergroup/User3
```

would list the contents of *User3*'s directory, which *ls* has sought out as a
file like any other. Likewise

```
$  ls ..
```

will list the contents of the directory directly above the current one and

```
$  ls .
```

will list the contents of the current directory (having the same effect as *ls* with no arguments).

Since directories are files, and vice versa, removing *subdir* should be simply a matter of applying *rm*;

```
$  rm subdir
rm:  subdir directory
```

rm has reported that *subdir* is a directory and refused to delete it. Deletion is one of the very few occasions when it becomes necessary to distinguish between files and directories, since consider what would happen if the subdirectory had contained files; deleting the directory would not delete the files contained therein, but they would be inaccessible since the node of the tree above them would no longer be present, meaning that there could no longer be a path to them. Removing directories needs explicit recognition of the fact that it is a directory to be removed; the command *rmdir* accomplishes this. *rmdir* is aware that it is dealing with directories and ensures they do not contain other files (which may, in turn, be directories) before performing the deletion. If *subdir* did contain files, we may see

```
$  rmdir subdir
rmdir:  subdir not empty
```

or

```
rmdir:  subdir:  Directory not empty
```

Before the deletion can happen, the directory must be emptied.

4.2 MORE FILE CHARACTERISTICS

We already know that files have *owners*, and have seen that a file may be a directory, or indeed a device. We need some way of interrogating a directory to discover the exact nature of the files it contains, to determine, say, who the owner is, or which are directories. The terse response of *ls* may be extended to do this job by employing one of its *options*.

Most Unix programs sport a variety of options which are specified on
the command line when wanted; usually they are single letters, and are
preceded by the hyphen character "-" to denote that they are options not
arguments; it is often the command-line options which differ most from
one version of Unix to another. *ls* provides the *-l* option which gives a
"long" directory listing. Compare the following;

```
$  ls
a.out
junk
mbox
prog.c
subd1
subd2
x

$  ls -l
total 34
-rwxr-xr-x 1 User      12728 May 1 12:29 a.out
-rw-r--r-- 1 User       2129 May 1 12:29 file1
-rw-r--r-- 1 User         17 May 1 12:29 junk
-rw-r--r-- 1 Another     84 May 1 12:29 prog.c
drwxr-xr-x 2 User        512 May 1 12:29 subd1
drwxr-xr-x 2 User        512 May 1 12:29 subd2
-rw-r--r-- 1 User          0 May 1 12:29 x
```

The *ls* command reveals the existence of seven files and no more; *ls −l*
provides a one line entry for each of these files which tells us considerably
more.

At the far right is the file name, directly preceded by its last modification date/time. To the left of the month of creation is an integer giving
the size in bytes of the file; for text files this is equal to the number of
characters in the file. Preceding file size is the name of the file owner;
files created by you may be expected to belong to you, but most of the
files around the system are going to belong to other people. In the example shown, a file called *prog.c*, belonging to user *Another* has found its
way into *User*'s directory. The integer before the owner's name refers to
the number of *links* to the file; we shall discuss links later in this chapter.
The first entry on the line is a ten (on some systems, eleven) character
string which defines the file's protection; that is, which other users may
access it. The first of these characters may have a variety of special meanings; most of these will not be discussed here beyond noting that if the
file is a directory, this first character is a "d". Thus *subd1* and *subd2* are

directories.

4.3 PROTECTIONS

The remaining nine characters are grouped into three groups of three which refer, respectively, to the file's owner, users in the same group as the owner, and all others. For each of these categories it is possible to specify the following access privileges:

r   - read access

w   - write access

x   - execute access

s   - set user-id privilege

t   - save text privilege

The last two will be of interest to sophisticated users and will be discussed in Chapter 9. To elaborate on the others, in the example shown *a.out* provides the *owner* (characters 2,3,4) with read, write and execute access, fellow *group* members with read and execute privilege, and all other users similarly with read and execute privilege.

Group membership, which is in the gift of system managers and administrators, normally binds you to other users involved in similar work or projects to yourself. On System V versions of Unix, you are normally in one group at any one time, although you may be allowed to switch between groups. On early versions of Berkeley Unix you can belong to up to eight groups simultaneously; under the most recent Berkeley release, 4.3, that has been increased to sixteen. The *groups* command will give you a list of the groups that you are in.

Likewise, the owner, her fellow group members and all other users have read access to *junk*, but only the owner may write to it. Execute privilege is not mentioned so it is fair to assume that the file is a text file and not in any sense executable.

Note now that a file may only be *deleted* by a user having write access to its directory; in the given example we have no way of knowing what this is. It is important to distinguish between the results of having write access to a *file* (which will allow a user to change the contents of the file) and having write access to a *directory* (which will allow a user to create and delete files in that directory). There is a slightly subtle but useful point relating to read and execute permissions on a directory; if you do not follow this explanation at first reading, please don't worry. If you have read permission on a directory, this implies that you can open the directory and search it — in other words, you can determine the contents of the directory. If you have execute permission on a directory, this implies that you can access a file that is in the directory. Therefore, if you have execute permission, but *not* read permission, you can access files that are in the directory *if you know that they are there.* A simple example may make this more clear.

```
$  ls -l
drwx------ 2 User    512 May 1 12:29 dir
$  ls -l dir
-rwxr-xr-x 1 User 12728 May 1 12:29 a.out
-rw-r--r-- 1 User  2129 May 1 12:29 file1
$  chmod u-r dir
$  ls -l
d-wx------ 2 User    512 May 1 12:29 dir
$  ls -l dir
dir unreadable
$  ls -l dir/a.out
-rwxr-xr-x 1 User 12728 May 1 12:29 a.out
```

It is also possible to have read permission on a directory without execute permission, but the authors have never been able to find a practical use for this facility.

Protections are a very useful way of allowing selected users to do selected things with your files; existing protections may be altered with the *chmod* (change mode) command. *chmod* needs to know whose access is to be changed, which access (r, w or x), whether it is to be added or removed, and of course which file(s) are to be reprotected. The "who" is specified by one of the following;

    u   - user (=owner)
    g   - group (the owning group)
    o   - other (=everybody else)
    a   - all of these

and adding/removing access is denoted by the characters +, − respectively. An example should help to clarify this; we shall toy with the protection of *junk* from the example above:

```
$  ls -l junk
-rw-r--r--  1  User  17  May  1  12:29  junk
$  chmod g+w junk
$  ls -l junk
-rw-rw-r--  1  User  17  May  1  12:29  junk
$  chmod a+x junk
$  ls -l junk
-rwxrwxr-x  1  User  17  May  1  12:29  junk
$  chmod a-w junk
$  ls -l junk
-r-xr-xr-x  1  User  17  May  1  12:29  junk
$  chmod o-x junk
$  ls -l junk
-r-xr-xr--  1  User  17  May  1  12:29  junk
$  rm junk
rm:   junk 554 mode
```

This enigmatic final message is *rm* telling us that an attempt has been made to delete *junk* without the necessary write privilege and *rm* has complained; if we had really wanted to delete the file, answering the remark in the affirmative (by typing *y*) would have done so. Note that *rm* has translated the nine character protection code into three octal digits. This correspondence is quite straightforward — interpreting the nine characters as binary digits, zeroes correspond to the dashes, and ones to occurrences of *r*, *w* and *x*. Many versions of Unix will provide a slightly more helpful response to such attempts at deletion — Berkeley Unix for example would respond

```
rm:   override protection 554 for x?
```

which makes it plain that a question is being asked.

It is valid to ask where protections come from; how, for instance, does a new file get its protection? Each user has a default protection, called *umask*, set up which determines this. *umask* thinks in the same octal notation as *rm* reported in, but (confusingly) takes its binary complement. (In other words, the *umask* indicates which protection bits are to be turned **off** when a file is created.) We can determine this default protection by issuing the command *umask*;

```
$  umask
022
```

Remember this is the binary complement of the protection, which decodes as 755, or

```
rwxr-xr-x
```

in character notation, thus giving all but write permission to all users (this is a very common default — another one is 002 which gives write permission to fellow group members as well). Changing the *umask* is simply a matter of giving the *umask* command an argument in the notation it understands. For instance

```
$   umask 77
```

would ensure that subsequently created files gave no-one except the owner any access. Unfortunately, the *umask* command does not understand the character notation for permissions — the octal notation must be used.

4.4 DEVICES

We have encountered the idea that Unix considers devices such as terminals, disks, tapes etc. to be files and may therefore expect to be able to look at their file attributes in much the same way as we would an ordinary text file. These device-files are usually lodged in the directory */dev* which may be interrogated with *ls -l* in the usual way. Each system has its own configuration of devices and so it is impossible to be precise about what may be found in */dev*, but it is certain that there will be an entry for each terminal and disk, together with any lineprinters, magnetic tape drives etc. that your particular installation sports.

One other device that will certainly be there is *null*, the null device. There will be a multitude of times when it is convenient to have either a way of creating an empty file, or a way of discarding output, and the null device provides this. *null*, or to give it its full pathname, */dev/null* is an empty file which Unix is prepared to accept as an input/output device. Thus for example

```
$   cp /dev/null emptyfile
```

will create for you an empty file, but

```
$   cat file >/dev/null
```

will not put the output of the *cat* operation into the *file /dev/null*, but into the *device /dev/null*, which is the equivalent of throwing it away. The null device functions as a universal dustbin, or black hole; it is a useful and oft-used facility.

Some specific entries in */dev* may look like;

```
$  ls -l /dev
.   .   .   .   .   .   .   .   .   .   .   .   .   .   .
crw-rw-rw- 1 root   3, 2 May 9 16:38 /dev/null
.   .   .   .   .   .   .   .   .   .   .   .   .   .   .
crw--w--w- 1 root   1, 0 May 9 17:04 /dev/tty00
crw--w--w- 1 You    1, 1 May 9 20:08 /dev/tty01
crw--w--w- 1 User1  1, 2 May 9 20:05 /dev/tty02
crw--w--w- 1 User2  1, 3 May 9 19:37 /dev/tty03
.   .   .   .   .   .   .   .   .   .   .   .   .   .   .
```

Note that the first character of the line for these entries is a *c*, denoting that the device is character structured; had we listed some disk devices, they would have appeared with a *b* indicating block structure. Of more interest is the ownership; bona fide shared devices, like disks and the null device, will usually be owned by *root* and be accessible only to *root* (although notice that everyone has read/write access to the null device). Terminals, however, are owned by whoever is using them; in the example, *You* are logged on at *tty01*, *User1* at *tty02*, *User2* at *tty03* and so on. Unattended terminals will usually register as owned by *root*. Observe that, perhaps surprisingly, all users have write access to your terminal; this permits them to send you messages while you are logged in that will appear on your terminal. You can of course, since you own the device, turn off this feature if you choose;

```
$  chmod go-w /dev/tty01
```

This feature is further discussed in Section 8.17 as the *mesg* command.

4.5 LINKS

We return to the topic of *links*. When listing a directory and seeing a collection of filenames, conceptually we think of those files living in that directory, and indeed on many computer systems that is the case. Unix however manages things differently; the directory entry acts as a *pointer* or *link* to the file, which is stored, with its attributes, at one remove from the user. This feature is invisible, and to all intents and purposes the file does "live" within your directory, but it does afford a convenient mechanism for users to share files.

Consider a situation in which *User1* owns and maintains a database to which *User2* requires access. Since *User2* expects it to be up to date at all times she will not be satisfied with taking a copy since *User1* might update the database and *User2*'s copy would then be out of date. A solution would be to access it explicitly by filename, but now there is no protection for *User2* if *User1* should decide to delete it, which, as owner, she will always be entitled to do. The *link* system provides a better solution. *User2* can *link* to the file in question; this will create an entry in *User2*'s directory and it will appear that *User2* has a copy of the file. Linking is accomplished by the *ln* command, used thus;

```
$   ln filename newfilename
```

which would produce a link to *filename* called *newfilename*.

Since the directory entry is just a link, or pointer, there is in fact only one copy of the file and any amendments made by *User1* will appear in the file which is pointed at by *User2*'s link. It is important to realise that the file is still *owned* by *User1*, as a directory listing by *User2* will show. Thus, despite the existence of the link, *User1* is still at liberty to take away *User2*'s read or write access to the file; the link does not imbue *User2* with any privilege she did not already have.

Now though, consider what will happen if *User1* deletes the file; *rm* does not, contrary to suggestion, delete the file, it merely severs the link. Thus if a file has more than one link, it remains intact at the deletion of one of them; *User2* will still have the directory entry (and file) intact, albeit still owned by *User1*. Only when a file's *last* link is deleted will the file itself be truly removed.

Remember now that when a *directory* appears in the output from *ls -l*, it shows two (or more) links; this is because the file which is the directory appears in its parent directory (by name) *and* in itself (as "."). In fact all newly created directories automatically contain two entries — themselves as "." and their parent as "..".

4.6 FILE SYSTEMS

At this point a brief digression is needed to explain a problem with links
that a user may meet — that of not being allowed to link between *file
systems*. A Unix system divides each disk drive that is connected to it
into a series of *partitions*; each partition occupies part (or all) of a disk,
and will have a device entry in the */dev* directory. For example, part of
the */dev* directory on this system is

```
$  ls -lg /dev/*xy*
. . . . . . . . . . .  . . . .
brw------- 1 root system 3,  0 Sep 20 09:46 /dev/xy0a
brw------- 1 root system 3,  1 Jan 26 1988 /dev/xy0b
brw------- 1 root system 3,  2 Jan 26 1988 /dev/xy0c
brw------- 1 root system 3,  3 Jan 26 1988 /dev/xy0d
brw------- 1 root system 3,  4 Jan 26 1988 /dev/xy0e
brw------- 1 root system 3,  5 Jan 28 1988 /dev/xy0f
brw------- 1 root system 3,  6 Jan 26 1988 /dev/xy0g
brw------- 1 root system 3,  7 Jan 26 1988 /dev/xy0h
. . . . . . . . . . . . . . .
```

Each of the entries is marked as a *block special* device; each of the
entries corresponds to a partition of a single disk. The partitions can
be any size from zero up to the total size of the disk. A file system is
stored in a partition — all of the information relating to a file system is
stored within one partition. A file system cannot be spread over multiple
partitions,[1] nor can a partition be spread over disks. A file is identified
within a file system by its *inode number* — these numbers begin at 2 (for
historical reasons) and go up to some suitably large number; the inode
numbering for each file system begins at 2. Each inode number tells Unix
where to find a block of information within the file system which contains
the file size, access permissions, owner identifier, and so on. The only
way of identifying a file uniquely is by its file system and inode number.

An entry in a directory consists of two items — the *file name* and
the *inode number*. As a result, a link cannot point to a file on another
file system — there is no way for a directory entry to indicate which
file system a file is on. It is not unreasonable to ask how Unix manages
to make all the file systems that are attached to one system look like a
single tree — what happens to the boundaries between the file systems?

---

[1]Some Unix implementations (such as AIX) allow file systems to be spread over
partitions and between disks. These are quite definite exceptions to the rule.

The answer is that a file system can be *mounted* on a directory using the *mount* command; once a file system has been mounted, then Unix makes the boundary largely invisible. In recent years, some Unix systems have begun to provide *symbolic links* which allow a user to create a link to another file by name — when a symbolic link is referenced, the file that is pointed at by the symbolic link is used. This allows links to be created between file systems. For more information on mounting and unmounting file systems, see Chapter 9 under *System Calls*.

4.7   THE SUPER-USER

All computer systems that support multi-user access need at least one *privileged* user; this will normally be a secure account held by the operator or system manager. On Unix systems, this user is called *root* (not to be confused with the *root* directory), to whom we have already referred once or twice. *root* wields all the god-like powers that such users may expect — she can override all user-set protections and has access to all the files and programs on the system, some of which may be confidential or potentially dangerous to the system's integrity.

root's power comes from possessing *super-user* privilege. Some operating systems will offer a whole range of privileges that users may qualify for, but Unix has just the one; with it, you can do nearly anything — without it you are restricted to normal user access and protections. *Super-user* privilege is password protected, and most users will never have it; we mention it since it is required in order to access some of the files and programs we describe in subsequent chapters, and because it is important to an understanding of some of the topics discussed in Chapter 9.

Chapter 5

The Bourne Shell Command Language

Up to now we have encountered several Unix commands, invoked by typing lines such as:

```
$   rm myfile
$   mv oldfile newfile
$   cat >inputfile
```

Whenever such a command is typed at the terminal, it is looked at by a program called the *shell*, which examines the line and decides which program should be run to carry out the command, and what arguments to pass to it; for example, if the line

```
$   rm myfile
```

is typed, the shell will decide that it needs to run a system program called *rm*, and pass it the single word *myfile* as argument.

The *arguments* of a program are strings of characters which are made available to the program when it is run. They are used to pass to it such information as the name of a file (to be edited, removed, typed out, or whatever the particular program chooses to do with it), the name of a user (as in the *passwd* command) or a list of command options (such as the "–l" option to the *ls* command).

In this chapter, we shall look more closely at the workings of the Bourne shell, and see some of the more powerful things which can be done with it, beyond the simple commands we have used so far. It should be borne in mind that, although the Bourne shell is common to all Unix systems (somewhat like *ed*), there are other shells available. Of these, the most common is the Berkeley *C-shell*, but other shells such as the Visual shell do exist. Some versions of System V provide the *Korn* shell, which is a strict superset of the Bourne shell.

5.1   THE COMMAND LINE

Whenever the shell is ready to read a command from the terminal, it types out a *prompt* to tell the user that it expects a command. On most Unix systems, this prompt is "*$*"; however, it is possible that your system may use a different prompt. If you are using Berkeley Unix, or a system derived from it, you may very well get the prompt "*%*"; in this case, you are probably not talking to the shell, but to the *C-shell*. The version of the Bourne shell described here was first laid down in Unix Version 7, and has changed relatively little since then. Much of the following discussion will apply equally to all of the command-line shells.

Almost all commands to the shell cause some program to be run; the program may be one of the standard programs which we describe as part of Unix, or it may be a program written by you or by someone else on your system. The name of the program to be run is the first word on your command line. Thus the command

```
$  cat myfile
```

causes the Unix program *cat* to be run, while the command

```
$  myprogram mydata
```

causes *myprogram* (presumably one of your programs) to be run. How, you may wonder, does the shell know where to find a program?

5.2   FINDING THE PROGRAM TO BE RUN

The program name you specify can be a full-blown Unix pathname, such as */bin/cat*, */usr/staff/jim/tidy* or *../progs/myprogram*. In these cases, recognised by the presence of a "*/*" in the name, the shell simply tries to find the file you have named and run it; of course, you will get error messages if the file does not exist, is not a valid program, or is protected against you. The most common messages take the form

```
../progs/myprogram:  not found
```

and

`../progs/myprogram:`   `Permission denied`

More often, the command will be a "simple" command-name, without any "/"s. In this case, the shell looks for the program in a series of directories in succession, running the first one it finds (if any); this series of directories is called your *path*, and we shall see later how you can set up your path to whatever you want. On most systems, your path will consist of (at least) three directories: your current directory ("."") and the two "system" directories */bin* and */usr/bin*. On Berkeley Unix systems, your path will probably have a number of additional directories such as */usr/ucb*, */usr/new* and */usr/hosts*. Most of the commands such as *cat*, *rm, ed* and so on are kept in */bin*; less commonly used commands live in */usr/bin*. The exact division of programs between these directories varies from system to system, as does the possible inclusion of other directories; a common feature is to include a subdirectory *bin* of your login directory, e.g. */usr/staff/jim/bin*, where you can keep your personal "vocabulary" of commands. It is worthwhile remembering that Unix is constantly being improved and updated — some recent versions have reduced the */bin* directory to a set of commands that are essential while the system is being reloaded; most of the remaining commands have been moved to the */usr/bin* directory.

5.3   EXPANDING THE COMMAND LINE

Before running the program you have asked for, the shell processes your command line to determine what arguments to pass to the program[1]. In simple cases, the arguments will simply be the sequences of non-blank characters on the command line; thus in the command

```
$  ls -l myfile myotherfile hisfile
```

the arguments will be the four text strings *-l, myfile, myotherfile* and *hisfile*. Space and tab characters between arguments are ignored; if you want to include a space or tab character in an argument, then it is necessary to surround the argument with quote-marks; they can be single or double (there *is* a difference, which we shall come to later), but the opening and closing quotes must match. Hence, you can type either of the following:

---

[1]Strictly speaking, this processing is done *before* determining which program to run.

```
$  echo "This argument contains 4 spaces"
$  echo 'This argument contains 4 spaces'
```

but if you type

```
$  echo "This argument contains 4 spaces'
```

the shell will not treat the final quote as matching the opening quote, and will respond with a ">" prompt, inviting you to complete the unfinished line of input.

Certain characters used in arguments to shell commands will not have the effect which you might naively expect; these are

$$< > | \tilde{} \& ; ? * [ ] ( ) \$ ` " ' \backslash \{ \}$$

We shall encounter all these in this and the next chapter; for the time being be warned not to use them simply to stand for themselves. If you *do* need to enter any of the special characters in a command argument, you can do so safely either by preceding them with the character "\" (*backslash*) or by placing them between matching quotation marks.

Many of the special characters affect the way that the command line is split into arguments; we shall look first at a group which is used to match filenames.

5.4   MATCHING FILENAMES - WILDCARD EXPANSION

The characters "*", "?" and "[...]" are *pattern-matching* characters, also known as *wildcard* characters.   Whenever one of them is used in a command, the argument is replaced by a list of *all* the filenames which match it, according to the following rules:

* * matches any sequence of zero or more characters. (This is *not* the same use of "*" as in *ex* and other programs, where it means "any number of occurrences of the preceding expression").

? matches any single character, just as "." does in *ex*.

[string] matches any one of the characters in *string*, again as in *ex*. The shell understands ranges such as *[a-z]* properly.

(To be pedantic, none of the above characters will match a "/" in a pathname; their view is restricted to a single directory at a time).

Suppose, for example, that the current directory contains the files:

doc.n list.c readme run.c run.n

Then the effect of the pattern matching characters can be seen in the following dialogue:

```
$  echo r*
read_me run.c run.n
$  echo *.c
list.c run.c
$  echo r*.[cn]
run.c run.n
$  echo ???????
read_me
$  ls [dr]*c*
doc.n run.c
```

Note that it is the *shell* which is doing all the pattern matching here; *ls* (in these examples) never sees the special characters at all, but only the lists which replace them.

The matches are not restricted to the current directory: the command

```
echo */tmp/*
```

will, for example, echo the names of all the files in each subdirectory called *tmp* of any directory in the current directory.

Filenames beginning with a dot are *excluded* from matches with the wildcard characters, just as they are excluded from directory listings unless you specifically ask for them. If you want to match *all* files in the current directory, you must specify

```
*  .*
```

This is because a number of Unix utilities make use of *start-up files* whose names begin a "."—for example, when the Bourne shell starts up it reads commands from the file *.profile* in your home directory (See section 6.12); there can be a great many of these files for various utilities in your home directory. By default, *ls* ignores such files when listing the contents of a directory, and wild-card expansion will not match them unless you explicitly ask for them by entering ".*".

5.5   REDIRECTED INPUT AND OUTPUT STREAMS

You have already met the special use of the characters ">" and "<"; they are used for *redirecting* the output and input of a program. Any command which you run will have access to three "standard" streams of data - the *standard input, standard output* and *standard error* streams; most programs, as you would expect, use these for their principal source of input, principal destination for output, and destination for error messages. When a command is started from the terminal, these streams will all normally be the terminal; however, they can be redirected to other files, or indeed to other programs. The simplest forms of redirection are exemplified below:

```
$   ls -l >directory-list
$   ed myfile <ed-script
```

The first of these places a directory listing in the file *directory-list*; if it already exists, it will be overwritten, and otherwise it will be created. The second runs *ed* with its input taken from the file *ed-script* rather than from the terminal; this can be used for carrying out some editing task which is needed frequently.

In addition to these simple redirections there are several other ways of redirecting the input or output streams; a full list is given in the Unix manual, but it is worth mentioning a few of them here. [2]

>>filename Append the standard output onto the end of the named file (if *filename* does not exist, this is just the same as > *filename*).

<< terminator Use the following lines as standard input, up to a line matching the given *terminator*; this is used in shell *scripts,* which are described in Chapter 6.

2 >*filename* Send standard error stream to *filename*; this is in fact a special case of a more general facility to associate a *file descriptor* with a file for input or output redirection. File descriptors will be discussed in Chapter 9. Please observe that there must be no space between the number of the file descriptor and the > sign.

---

[2]The forms of redirection available differ somewhat between the C-shell and the Version 7/System V Bourne shell; it is the last of these which we describe here.

Note that these redirections are handled by the shell itself; the redirection symbols are *not* included in the list of arguments passed to the program to be executed, which in consequence does not, in general, know the name of its standard input or output, nor indeed whether they are disk files, terminals, or pipes to other programs, as described in the next section.

5.6 PIPELINES

A form of redirection which is particularly useful, and forms an essential part of the vocabulary of every experienced Unix user, is the *pipeline*. In a pipeline, two or more programs are run together, with the output from one being passed as input to the next. On most implementations of Unix the programs in a pipeline are executed *concurrently*, that is, in effect, simultaneously. The main advantage of the pipeline, from the user's point of view, is that it provides a concise notation for the sort of task which would require the use of temporary files on many other systems. Consider the following example, which uses the document preparation programs described in Chapter 11:

```
$  refer myfile >tempfile-1
$  tbl <tempfile-1 >tempfile-2
$  neqn <tempfile-2 >tempfile-3
$  nroff -ms <tempfile-3 >tempfile-4
$  lpr <tempfile-4
```

This uses four temporary files, which are left in the current directory at the end, and is much less compact than its pipeline equivalent:

```
$  refer myfile | tbl | neqn | nroff -ms | lpr
```

This has exactly the same final output, but does not create any temporary files and runs the five commands in parallel. On a single-processor machine the commands will share the available processing power. On a multiple processor machine, however, the second form of the command is a definite advantage — the commands will probably be executed on more than one processor, allowing for considerably faster execution of the whole command.

As you will see, the pipeline symbol is a vertical bar, "|". It separates a pair of commands; the output of the command on the left of the bar is passed as input to the command on the right; as the example shows, a whole series of commands can be run together in this way.

The reason that the pipeline is so useful in a Unix system is because there is a large collection of Unix tools, known as *filters*, that take a stream of input, manipulate it in some way, and pass the resulting stream of data to their standard output. Indeed, one of the central ideas behind Unix was to implement commands as filters wherever possible; this allows complex commands to be constructed in a "tool-kit" manner using existing commands. Pipelines make it possible to build powerful data-manipulation commands by plugging together a series of filters. We shall encounter many of these tools in Chapters 7 and 11.

5.7 BACKGROUND EXECUTION OF COMMANDS

We have seen that the Unix system is capable of performing many tasks concurrently; it can handle many simultaneous users, and it can run multi-command pipelines for a single user. In addition, a user can explicitly run several independent commands at the same time; this is done by running *background* commands.

Usually, after each command is entered the shell runs the corresponding program, and then waits for it to finish; it is possible to ask the shell to start the program, but not to wait for its completion before accepting another command. This is shown by ending the command to be run in the background with "&" (ampersand). Many commands can be run simultaneously in this way, though there is usually some limit imposed by the system on the maximum number of simultaneous tasks a user is allowed to run; even if you are working on a machine by yourself, creating a great many background tasks will tend to slow the system down appreciably. In the following example

```
$  cc myprogram.c&
9138
$  ed newprogram.c
```

the shell prompts for the second command as soon as the first command (a request to compile a C program) is entered, even though the compilation may not finish for some time. The number which the shell prints out when you run a background command is its *process number* or *process id*. You can use this in commands such as *kill*, described in Chapter 8.

When running several commands, it is possible to get confused by the overlapping of their output. Even more confusing, it is sometimes possible for several programs to try to read input from your terminal at the same time; each line you type will go to one of them, but it is virtually impossible to predict which! The best way to avoid such problems is not to run interactive programs in the background; redirect their output to a file, and make them read their input, if any, from another file. An alternative solution, if you are using a Berkeley Unix system or one of its variants, is to use the elegant *job control* facilities of the C-shell, which enable you to run many interactive tasks at once. These will be mentioned in Chapter 10.

5.8 COMMAND GROUPING

There are a few other pieces of punctuation used by the shell to separate commands or group them together; some of these are keywords like *if*, *then*, *else* and *while*. We shall look at these in Chapter 6, where we consider the shell as a programming language. In addition, there are the following:

    ; ( ) ‖ &&

We will only consider the semicolon and parentheses in this chapter.

A semicolon is used to end one command and start another on the same line, e.g.

```
$  date; ls; echo Ready
Sun Jul 10 15:21:38 GMT 1983
myfile
myprogram.c
newprogram.c
Ready
$
```

The shell does not prompt for another command until it has executed all of the commands separated by semicolons.

Sometimes you will want to execute a sequence of commands in the background. Typing

```
$  date; ls; echo Ready&
```

will not achieve the desired result, but will instead run first *date*, and then *ls*, and only then will the single command *echo Ready* be run as a background command. To group commands together, you can use parentheses, so that a sequence of commands can be run in the background by typing

```
$   (date; ls; echo Ready)&
```

5.9 SUMMARY

This chapter has introduced many of the features of the shell as an interactive command language; however, it has many more features which make it usable as a programming language, with conditional execution, loops, variables, and so on. These features will be described in the next chapter.

Chapter 6

The Shell as a Programming Language

The shell is not merely an interactive command language. It is also a programming language, in which new commands can be written in terms of existing Unix commands. In this chapter we shall look at command *scripts* written using the shell. [1]

A shell script is simply a file containing a sequence of shell commands; anything which is valid when using the shell interactively from a terminal can be placed in a script, and *vice versa*, but some shell features are far more useful in scripts than interactively.

6.1   CREATING AND EXECUTING A SHELL SCRIPT

A script is created simply by creating a file containing the desired sequence of commands. It can be executed in two ways: by specifying it explicitly as the input file to the shell, which is invoked as the command *sh*, e.g.

```
$  sh myscript
```

or

```
$  sh < myscript
```

(the shell reads from a named file if given one as argument, otherwise from its standard input); or by simply typing the name of the file, e.g.

```
$  myscript
```

or

---

[1]The C-shell is also a programming language, which differs substantially in many features from the System III/System V shell described here. We shall look briefly at the C-shell in Chapter 7.

```
$  ./myscript
```

In order for the second method to work, you must have *execute* permission for the file, set by the *chmod* command, e.g.

```
$  chmod u+x myscript
```

If you wish to try an example, we would suggest that you avoid the use of the name *test*; there is a command called *test*, and you may not get the results that you expect. When the shell tries to execute a command, it first checks that you have execute permission, and if so, it checks whether the command is an executable program or a shell script (using a flag called the *magic number* in the first two bytes or four bytes of an executable file). If it is a script, the shell starts up a new copy of itself to read and carry out the command script. Thus, command scripts can be invoked in precisely the same way as compiled programs written in C, FORTRAN, or any other available language. Berkeley versions of Unix sometimes allow shell scripts to run alternative programs by putting a line like

> #!/bin/csh
> *text of shell script*

at the very beginning of the file. The "#!" is treated as a "magic number", and the string following it is treated as the name of a program to run — in this case, */bin/csh*. In general, the full path name of any Unix command can appear after the "#!" — this results in the command being executed, with the contents of the command file being fed to it *via* the standard input. This facility evolved slowly from one Berkeley system to another, so it may not be fully available on all systems. (For example, some early Berkeley systems simply treated the characters "#!" at the beginning of a file as a request to use the C-Shell instead of the Bourne shell.)

6.2 VARIABLES AND PARAMETERS

The shell allows the use of *variables* to contain numeric or string values. Unlike many languages, there is no need to declare variables before use; a variable can be created simply by assigning a value to it, and if a variable is used before receiving a value, it is assumed to contain an empty string, i.e. one consisting of no characters. Assignment appears as

```
$   NAME=chris
$   BIRTHDAY='December 1st'
```

which assigns the strings "chris" and "December 1st" to the variables NAME and BIRTHDAY. Note that, as elsewhere in the shell, you need to enclose a value containing spaces or special characters in quotation marks. To *substitute* the value of a variable into a command line, the variable-name is preceded with a dollar character, "*$*". Assuming the above assignments, then the following two commands are precisely equivalent:

```
$   echo $NAME was born on $BIRTHDAY
chris was born on December 1st
$   echo chris was born on December 1st
chris was born on December 1st
```

Without a preceding "*$*", the shell does not recognise the variable name as in any way special:

```
$   echo NAME was born on BIRTHDAY
NAME was born on BIRTHDAY
```

The shell has several "special" variables, which are automatically set up for you, and which have special meanings:

HOME is the pathname of your "home" directory, initially set up to be your login directory. This is the directory that becomes current whenever you use the *cd* command without an argument. You are allowed to alter the value of HOME from its original value.

PATH contains a series of directory names separated by colons; this is the list of places where the shell looks for files to execute when you type a command. Typically it will look something like

```
/usr/staff/andrew/bin:/bin:/usr/bin:.
```

which will cause the shell to search the subdirectory "*bin*" of andrew's login directory, the two "system" directories */bin* and */usr/bin* and the current directory ".". You are allowed to alter the value of PATH to include extra directories, exclude directories, or change the order of searching. For example,

```
PATH=$PATH:/usr/local
```

will add the directory /usr/local to the end of the existing search path.

Since the directories in the search path are scanned in the order in which they appear, it is advisable to put the current directory "." at the **end** of the path list — otherwise, as you move around the file system, there is always a risk of typing the name of a conventional system command, only to find that you have executed a command of the same name in the current directory.

PS1 contains the shell's prompt, usually set to "$ " initially. You can change this to anything you like, for example

```
$  PS1='Ready when you are, Sir:  '
Ready when you are, Sir:
echo hello
hello
Ready when you are, Sir:
```

PS2 is the continuation prompt written out by the shell when a command extends over more than one line, initially ">".

$ is the process number of the current shell; you cannot change this.

! is the process number of the background command started most recently from the current shell; this is useful for commands such as *kill*.

? is the *exit status* of the previous command; we shall describe exit status in the section on Flow of Control.

1-9 are the command arguments with which the script was called; for example when running the script *myscript* with the command

```
$  myscript chris staff 'December 1st'
```

"$1" is replaced throughout *myscript* by "chris", "$2" by "staff" and "$3" by "December 1st".

0 is the name with which the script was called; in the previous example, "$0" would be replaced by "myscript".

* is replaced by a list of all the arguments of the script; in the previous example "$*" would be replaced by "chris staff December 1st".

is the number of arguments in the command line, 3 in the above example.

Another way to set a shell variable is by using the shell command *read*, which reads a line from the standard input (usually the terminal) and assigns it to a variable; this is useful in interactive scripts:

```
echo "What program do you want to compile?"
read NAME
cc $NAME
```

The Bourne shell also provides the *shift* command for manipulating the parameter list; after a *shift* operation, the parameters are shifted down by one position — $2 becomes $1, $3 becomes $2, $4 becomes $3, ... etc. An example of the use of *shift* is given at the end of this chapter.

6.3   STANDARD INPUT AND OUTPUT

The standard input and output of a shell script are, as with other commands, inherited from the shell which started it running. So if you start a shell script from the terminal, and do not ask explicitly for any redirection, the standard input and output will be the terminal. Hence, the standard input and output of any programs started within the script will also be the terminal, unless the script specifies a redirection.

It is often desirable to include the input for a command within a script itself; this can be done using the "<<" redirection mentioned in Chapter 5, which defines a *here document*. The "<<" is followed by any word you like, and all subsequent text in the script up to a line consisting only of that word will be read as the standard input of the command. For example, a script might contain

```
ed - $1 << 'End-of-ed'
1,$s/Sometimes/Never/g
w
q
End-of-ed
```

which will replace all occurrences of the word "Sometimes" in the file named as first argument of the script by "Never" (the option "-" to *ed* makes it suppress printing the character counts before and after editing). In this example the script contained a "*$*" which we did not want to be treated as flagging a variable to be substituted. We indicated that no substitution was to take place within the input for *ed* by *quoting* the terminating word. If it is left unquoted, then variable and command substitution (described below) *will* take place, which is frequently useful, as in

```
ed - $1 << End-of-ed
1,\$s/$2/$3/g
w
q
End-of-ed
```

which will replace all occurrences of the string given as second argument of the script by its third argument. Note that we have had to escape the "*$*" line-number by placing a "\" in front of it, to prevent the shell trying to substitute the current value of variable *s* for "*$s*".

6.4   FLOW OF CONTROL

Like many other programming languages, the shell includes constructs for *loops* and *conditional* execution of commands. The loop constructs are *for*, *while*, and *until*. The conditional constructs are *if* and *case*.

if makes use of the *exit status* of a command; every command which you run returns a numeric value when it finishes; the standard convention is that an exit status of 0 corresponds to normal termination, while any non-zero value means that something went wrong, or that something unusual occurred. Several programs have been specially written to test for some condition, and exit with values of 0 or non-zero depending on whether the condition holds or not.

The format of an *if* statement is

```
if command
then
      sequence of commands
elif
      command
then
      sequence of commands
      ...
else
      sequence of commands
fi
```

If the first command exits with status 0, then the first sequence of commands is executed, and the rest skipped. Otherwise, the command in the *elif* part is run, and if it exits with status 0, the corresponding sequence of commands is executed, and so on down to the *else* part, whose sequence of commands is run only if all the earlier tests return non-zero. The *elif* and *else* parts are optional; if there is no *else* part and the test returns non-zero, the shell ignores the remainder of the *if* statement. For example

```
if grep -s $NAME namelist
then
      echo $NAME is OK
else
      echo I have never heard of $NAME
fi
```

looks for an occurrence of the value of the variable NAME in a file called *namelist*, and echoes a different message depending on whether or not it is present (the program *grep* will be described in Chapter 8).

One of the most commonly used conditions in an *if* statement is the program *test*. This can be used to test whether a file exists, is readable, or writeable, whether two strings are the same, or whether one number is greater than, equal to, or less than another, and so on. The full range of options of *test* is described in the Unix Programmer's Manual; an example should suffice to illustrate its use.

```
if test -r messagefile
then
     if test -w summaryfile -a -w messagefile
     then
           cat messagefile >> summaryfile
           cp /dev/null messagefile
     else
           echo cannot write to summary or message file
     fi
else
     echo cannot read messagefile
fi
```

This will append the contents of *messagefile* onto the end of *summaryfile* and make *messagefile* empty provided that *messagefile* is readable and both files are writable, and will otherwise print a suitable message. This example also shows that it is possible to nest one *if* statement inside another.

The other conditional statement is the *case* statement; this corresponds to the multi-way conditional branches such as *switch* in C and *case* in Pascal and Algol 68. The format is

```
case word in
     pattern₁₁| pattern₁₂| ...)
           command-sequence₁
           ;;
     pattern₂₁| pattern₂₂| ...)
           command-sequence₂
           ;;
esac
```

The specified *word* is matched successively against each of the patterns, and as soon as a match is found, the corresponding command-sequence is executed. Note especially that each command-sequence is ended by a *double* semicolon. The patterns are exactly the same as the patterns used by the shell to match filenames. Alternative patterns for the same command-sequence are separated by a vertical bar, "|". For example

```
case $OPTION in
    -p|-P)
            print $FILE
            ;;
    -[nN])
            nroff $FILE
            ;;
    *)
            echo unknown option $OPTION
            ;;
esac
```

Note that the final pattern "*" acts as a catch-all to pick up anything which does not match an earlier pattern, and that we have shown two different ways of matching an upper or lower-case OPTION — by giving either two alternative patterns, or else a single pattern to match either.

Loops can be written using a *while* (or *until*) loop, which repeatedly runs a command, tests its exit status, and if it is 0 (non-zero for an *until* loop) executes a corresponding command-sequence; when the status becomes non-zero (0 for *until*) the shell moves on to the statement following the loop. The format is

```
while command
do
    command-sequence
done

until command
do
    command-sequence
done
```

For example

```
REPLY=yes
while test "$REPLY" = "yes"
do
        echo "Here we go again!"
        echo "Do you want to go round the"
        echo " loop another time?"
        read REPLY
done
```

The final looping construct is *for*, which looks like

```
for variable-name in word-list
do
    command-sequence
done
```

The *command-sequence* is executed once for each word in *word-list*, with the named variable taking on successive values from *word-list*. The list of words can be generated using the wildcard filename matching of the shell; it can also be omitted completely, in which case it is taken to be the list of arguments with which the shell was started (i.e. *$**). For example

```
for file in *
do
    echo $file
    mv $file $file.old
done

for argument
do
    ed $argument
done
```

6.5 COMMENTS

You can include comments in your shell scripts by using the command ":" or the "#" character; the ":" is a command which does nothing, so that its arguments may be used to provide commentary on the script. All of the shell's juggling with your command line — parameter substitution, wildcard matching, and so on — is done on the arguments of ":", so that they must satisfy the same syntax as is required by the shell for normal commands. A safe form of comment, though unappealing to the eye, is to enclose the entire comment text in single quotation marks, as in

```
#!/bin/sh
:  'are there too few arguments?'
if test $# -lt 3
then
     echo Not enough arguments
     exit 1

:  '...or too many?'
elif test $# -gt 5
then
     echo Too many arguments
     exit 2
fi
```

The foregoing example introduces a new shell command, *exit*. This terminates execution of the script, and uses its argument as the exit status; if omitted it is assumed to be zero. Hence we can use non-zero arguments to *exit* to indicate different sorts of failure to whatever program (usually the shell) started the command script running.

6.6   COMMAND SUBSTITUTION

It is possible to build up part of a command line by running some other command. If a command enclosed in grave accents (" ` ") is incorporated in a command line, then it is executed and its standard output, with line-feeds replaced by spaces, spliced into the command line in its place. The command inside graves can be any legal command, even a pipeline. For example the command

```
$  echo `ls | sort -r`
```

will echo a list of files in the current directory in reverse alphabetical order.

As you will probably realise, this is a very powerful feature, which can, however, lead to obscure scripts unless used with care.

6.7   ORDER OF EVENTS

In order to understand complex scripts, it is necessary to know in what order the shell carries out its various substitutions.

1. Parameter and variable substitution is carried out; all occurrences of "$" followed by a name, digit, or one of the special variable names such as "*" are substituted for unless the "$" is inside *single* quotation marks or preceded by a "\ ".

2. Command substitution (commands enclosed in graves) is carried out, unless the grave occurs within *single* quotes or preceded by "\ ". Thus, both these substitutions *do* take place inside double quotes; this constitutes the difference between single and double quotes mentioned in the previous chapter.

3. Filename substitution ("*", "?" and "[...]") takes place, unless the special characters are enclosed in *either* sort of quotation mark or preceded by "\ ".

6.8   OPTIONS TO THE SHELL

When the shell is invoked explicitly by the command *sh,* it is possible to pass various options to control its execution. The most useful of these are:

-e Exit as soon as any command in the script fails.

-v Verbose mode; print each input line as it is read.

-x Print commands as they are *executed.*

-n Read commands, but do not execute them.

Options can also be turned on within a script by the command *set,* e.g.

```
set -vx
```

to turn on verbose mode and execution tracing.

6.9   TRAPPING INTERRUPTS

In some scripts it is useful to be able to clean up in the event of something occurring which would normally cause execution to be abandoned, such as the user typing an interrupt or quit character. The command *trap* achieves this; it takes the form

```
trap action event-list
```

The *event-list* is a list of integers corresponding to Unix *signals*, as described in Chapter 8, with the value 0 specially interpreted as meaning "exit from the shell". The *action* is a command to be executed whenever a signal from the *event-list* occurs. If the action is an empty string, the corresponding events are ignored. The most useful signals are:

0 Exit from the shell

2 Interrupt from the terminal

3 Quit from the terminal

15 Terminate signal received

Thus if it is required to remove a temporary file when a script either exits normally or is interrupted, the following would do the job:

```
trap "echo Interrupted; exit" 2 3
trap "rm /tmp/tmpfile" 0
```

6.10 THE ENVIRONMENT

All processes on Unix (except old and distinctly rare versions) possess an *environment*, which is a collection of names with associated string values. When the shell is started up, it takes its initial environment to be a list of shell variables and their initial values. Furthermore, it passes its environment on to any commands which it invokes. However, any new variables created within a shell are *not* normally included in the environment; if you wish so to include them, you must explicitly request this with the command *export*.

```
$  export NAME BIRTHDAY
```

will add the variables NAME and BIRTHDAY to the current shell's environment, which will be inherited by any commands which it invokes. You should note that this is a one-way process; changing the environment of a shell or other program will have no effect whatsoever on the environment of the shell or program which invoked it.

There is a somewhat clumsy way of altering a shell's environment from a sub-program; this uses the command *eval*. *eval* simply evaluates its arguments as though they constituted a shell command line; thus if a program *name* writes, say, "NAME=chris" to its standard output, then the command

```
$  eval `name`
```

is equivalent to

```
$  NAME=chris
```

and thus has the effect of setting the shell variable NAME. Alternatively, it is possible to "splice" a script into the input of the current shell instead of starting a sub-shell to read it, using the command ". ".

```
$  . setup
```

will include the contents of the file *setup* in the input stream of the current shell just as though they had been part of the original input.

Sometimes you may want an environment variable to be set, but not subsequently alterable. This can be done by the command *readonly*:

```
readonly NAME BIRTHDAY
```

will cause the shell to report an error if you subsequently try to assign new values to either of the variables NAME or BIRTHDAY.

6.11 SHELL FUNCTIONS

Recent versions of the Bourne shell allow you to define *shell functions* in your shell scripts. These take the form

name() { *list of commands;* }

Unlike shell scripts, shell functions are executed by the current shell — the shell does not execute a shell function as a separate process. As a result, shell functions execute more quickly than shell scripts, and they can modify the environment of the current shell. Parameters to a shell function are available in exactly the same way as parameters to a shell script — as "$1", "$2", etc. For example,

```
chdir()
{
#
# chdir - change PS1 prompt to echo
# working directory
#
    if [ $# -lt 1 ]
        then cd
        else cd $1
    fi

    if [ "`pwd`" = "$HOME" ]
        then PS1='$'
        else PS1="`pwd | sed s?$HOME/??`"
    fi
}
```

In this example, the *[* command has been used in place of the *test* command — many Unix systems allow you to write test expressions in the form *[$# -lt 1]* instead of the equivalent form *test $# -lt 1*.

Shell functions are particularly useful for creating command *aliases*.

6.12 STARTING THE SHELL FROM *login*

When you first login to Unix, the program starts up a shell [2] for you; this shell, before reading from the terminal, will look in your login directory for a file called *.profile*, and if it exists, will read and execute commands from it. This allows you to set up your own environment, run any programs you want, and so on. A typical *.profile* might be

```
PATH=:$HOME/bin:/etc:/bin:/usr/bin
USER=andrew
MAIL=/usr/spool/mail/$USER
export PATH USER MAIL

# prevent other users from writing to the terminal
mesg n
# set default file creation mask
umask 027
```

---

[2]Usually; on some systems you may get a C-shell, and certain classes of user may run some other program altogether; see Chapter 9.

```
echo People currently logged on:
who

echo "Hello andrew; nice to see you again"
```

(although most people would rapidly get tired of such a chatty greeting!). The *.profile* can also be used to define shell functions, as described above.

6.13   AN EXAMPLE

There are still some subtleties of the shell which we have not described; if you want the full details you should refer to the Programmer's Manual, which gives a complete list of options and commands. We conclude this chapter with an example of a real shell script.

The script, *cptree*, makes a copy of an entire directory hierarchy; on many systems this is available as a standard program, with many more options than this simple script, but this version should serve as a reasonable example of elementary shell programming.

```
# Copy a directory hierarchy
# With optional argument '-v' echo filenames
if test "$1" = -v
then
      ECHO=echo
      VERBOSE=-v
      shift
      # replaces $1 by $2, $2 by $3, etc
else
      ECHO=:
fi
if test $# -ne 2
then
      echo usage: cptree from to
      exit 1
fi
# if first argument is a directory copy
# all files to second argument
if test -d $1
then
      if test -f $2
      then
            # second argument exists, but is not a directory
            echo cptree:  $2 is not a directory
            exit 1
      elif test !  -d $2
            # second argument does not exist - create it
      then
            $ECHO mkdir $2
            # Will echo the command if -v
            # was set, otherwise just a comment
            mkdir $2
      fi
      for FILE in `ls -a $1`
      # To make sure we get files beginning
      # with ``.''
      do
            if test $FILE = .  -o $FILE = ..
            then
                  # ignore this directory and
                  # parent directory
                  continue
            fi
            # call cptree recursively, passing on VERBOSE option
```

```
        cptree $VERBOSE $1/$FILE $2/$FILE
    done
elif test -r $1
then
    # just copy a non-directory
    $ECHO cp $1 $2
    cp $1 $2
else
    echo cptree:  cannot read $1
    exit 1
fi
```

Chapter 7

The C-Shell as a Command and
Programming Language

When the BSD project at the University of California at Berkeley issued
their version of Unix, one of the major additions was the *C-Shell*. It was
designed as an alternative to the Bourne shell, but was designed to include
facilities for *job control* — that is, the ability to move programs between
the foreground and the background. (In order for the C-Shell to provide
job control, however, it is necessary for the underlying version of Unix
to support it.)

Like the Bourne shell, the C-Shell provides the user with a command
language and a programming language; whereas the Bourne shell command language is designed to look like the language *Algol*, the C-Shell
is designed to look like the language *C*. The basic command language
of the C-Shell is very similar to that of the Bourne shell, although the
keywords and command structures differ.

7.1 MATCHING FILENAMES

The C-Shell supports all of the wildcard characters described on page 74,
but it provides two additional facilities for *generating* file names. The first
is the "˜" character, which is used to generate a user's login directory. By
itself, the "˜" expands to the login directory of the current user; if it is
suffixed by a user's name, it generates that user's login directory.

```
%  whoami
andrew
%  echo ˜
/usr/users/staff/andrew
%  echo ˜pete
/usr/users/research/pete
```

The parentheses "{}" can contain a comma-separated list of possible file
names, for example:.

```
*.{aux,doc,lib,dvi}
```

will match any filename in the current directory that ends in one of the strings "aux", "doc", "lib" or "dvi".

Unlike the wildcards that were described above, the "{}" characters generate file names; that is, an expression of the form

```
*.{aux,dvi}
```

will be expanded by the C-Shell into

```
*.aux *.dvi
```

For example, compare the results of the following commands:

```
$  echo *
data-file fix.c fix.h makefile patch.c patch.h
$  echo *.*
fix.c fix.h patch.c patch.h
$  echo rubbish.*
No match.
$  echo file.{dvi,aux,lib}
file.dvi file.aux file.lib
```

With the first *echo*, the shell will expand the "*" to all the files in the current directory that do not begin with "."; in the second example, "*.*" will match any file name that contains an embedded "." (notice that the "." in "*.*" will not match a "." at the beginning of a file name); in the final example, the "file.{...}" expression generates file names rather than matching them — hence the output from *echo*. Note that the shell does *not* sort the names that are generated before passing them to *echo* as arguments.

7.2 VARIABLES

The C-Shell makes a clear distinction between *environment variables* and *C-Shell variables. environment variables* are created and changed using the *setenv* command, and destroyed using the *unsetenv* command; for example,

```
%  setenv VAR "this is a string"
%  echo $VAR
this is a string
%  unsetenv VAR
%  echo $VAR
VAR: Undefined variable.
```

When a new program is run from the C-Shell, all of the environment variables that are currently defined are passed to the environment of the new program; unlike Bourne shell variables, it is not necessary to ask for them to be exported (see page 93).

C-Shell variables are created and destroyed using the *set* and *unset* commands; for example,

```
%  set var="this is a string"
%  echo $var
this is a string
%  unset var
%  echo $var
var:  Undefined variable.
```

Notice that the *set* command requires a "=" after the name of the variable, whereas the *setenv* command does not.

C-Shell variables are *local* to the environment of a C-Shell — they are not exported when a new program is run. By convention, C-Shell variables are written entirely in lower case, while environment variables are written entirely in upper case. You can list all of the current C-Shell and environment variables using the *set* and *printenv* commands; for example:

```
%   set
argv     ()
cwd      /usr/users/staff/andrew
history 30
home     /usr/users/staff/andrew
path     (/usr/bin /usr/ucb /usr/local/bin .)
...
%   printenv
EDITOR=emacs
HOME=/usr/users/staff/andrew
PATH=/usr/bin:/usr/ucb:/usr/local/bin:.
SHELL=/bin/csh
...
```

Some C-Shell variables are closely associated with a corresponding environment variable — when such a C-Shell variable is changed to a new value, the corresponding environment variable is updated as well. Examples include the search path for commands (which appears in the example above as the C-Shell variable *path* and the environment variable *PATH*), the home directory (*home* and *HOME*) and the type of the terminal that you are using (usually *term* and *TERM*). C-Shell variables such as *path* in the example above can be treated as *vectors* of items — you can select items from a vector using the notation:

```
$var[n]
```

You can use the notation

```
$#var
```

to determine the number of words in any variable. For example,

```
%   echo $path
/usr/bin /usr/ucb /usr/local/bin .
%   echo $#path
4
%   echo $path[2]
/usr/ucb
```

Unlike most versions of the Bourne Shell, the C-Shell maintains a lookup table of all the commands on the current search path in the form of a *hash list.* If you add a new command to one of the directories in your search path (for example, the *bin* directory in your login directory) you may have to rebuild this hash list. The C-Shell provides the *rehash* command for precisely this purpose.

7.3   THE DIRECTORY STACK

In addition to the *cd* command, the C-Shell provides the user with a push-down list (or *stack*) of directories. The top item on the directory stack is always the current directory, and the *cd* command will not only change the user's current directory but will also change the item on the top of the stack.

The C-Shell provides two commands to manipulate the directory stack; the *pushd* command to add directories to the top of the stack and the *popd* command to remove directories from the stack. The *dirs* command provides the user with a list of the current contents of the directory stack. When the user enters a *pushd* command, she moves to the named directory. When the user issues a *popd* command, the top item on the stack is discarded (unless there is only one item on the stack, in which case an error message appears) and the new top-of-stack item becomes her current directory. If the user enters the *pushd* command without a directory name, the top two items on the directory stack are exchanged; this is a very convenient technique for moving rapidly and repeatedly between two directories.

For example,

```
%  pwd
/usr/users/staff/andrew
%  dirs
~
%  pushd /tmp
/tmp  ~
%  pwd
/tmp
%  pushd
  swap the top two stack items
~  /tmp
%  popd
/tmp
```

7.4   THE HISTORY LIST

One of the most useful features supported by the C-Shell is the *history list*; the C-Shell keeps a list of the commands that you have entered, allowing you to recall them and edit them. The C-Shell variable *history*, which appears in the example above, indicates the number of items that are kept on the history list — as you type commands, they are appended to the end of the list and the old commands disappear. If *history* is not set, or is set to zero, there will be no history list. A possible history list would be:

```
%  history
50        latex chap6-1
51        texx -1 1 chap6-1
52        ls *.dvi
53        ls *.tex
...
```

The number that appears at the beginning of the line is the command number — it allows you to refer to previous commands by their number. The remaining text on the line is the body of the command that you typed. As commands are appended to the end of the history list the command number is incremented — if, for example, you have entered 150 commands and your *history* variable is set to 50, the history list will begin with the 101st command and end with the 151st (the *history* command itself). To re-run a previous command, the "!" command is used. If we assume the history list from the earlier example, we could issue the command:

```
%  !50
latex chap6-1
...output from latex ...
%
```

Here, the C-Shell retrieves item 50 from the history list and echoes it before executing it. The "!" command can retrieve commands from the history list in a number of different ways. The most common examples are:

!! Refer to the previous command.

!*n* Refer to the *n*th command, where *n* is a number.

!-*n* Refer to the current command minus *n*, where *n* is a number.

!*str* Refer to the most recent command that begins with *str*.

!?*str* Refer to the most recent command that contained the string *str*.

Hence, if command number 50 in the earlier example was the most recent invocation of the *latex* command, we could also have typed

```
%  !latex
latex chap6-1
...output from latex ...
%
```

The C-Shell history mechanism includes a number of powerful commands for editing the history list. For a full explanation, you should consult a tutorial on the C-Shell or else the C-Shell manual page. The most commonly used editing functions are as follows.

Word Designators

The C-Shell allows you to extract individual words, or groups of words, from a previous command by using *word designators*. A word designator is separated from the event specification by a colon (':'); the following list of word designators is not complete, but you may find it useful.

0 The 0th word of a command — in other words, the command name itself.

n The *n*th argument of a command.

$ The last argument of a command.

n-m A range of words; 1-$ will return all of the arguments to the command, if there were any.

* All of the arguments, from 1 to $; this is a shorthand notation for 1-$. It is legal to use this if there are no arguments, in which case it returns an empty string.

The following examples should make the use of these designators apparent.

```
%  history
50        cc -o image image.c fn1.c libim.a
51        image data1 data2 data3
52        lpr -v data3
53        lpr image.c
54        interpolate image1 image2
...
%  !int:0 image3
interpolate image3
...output from interpolate ...
%  lpr -v !:$
lpr -v image3
%  lpr !cc:3-4
lpr image.c fn1.c
%
```

Modifiers

The history mechanism also provides a set of *modifiers*; modifiers appear after the optional word designator and each modifier must be preceded by a colon (':'). Modifiers allow you to refer to previous commands and edit them before re-submitting them. The following list of modifiers is, like the word designator list, incomplete but useful.

p   Print the new command, but do not execute it. This is useful for confirming that a command is correct before executing it.

s/l/r/   Substitute the first occurrence of the string *l* in the word by the string *r*. If the word designator is missing, the substitution is performed on the first occurrence of *l* in the entire command.

g   Perform a substitution globally — each occurrence of the string *l* in a word or command will be replaced by the string *r*.

h   Remove a trailing pathname from a file name, leaving only the head.

t   Remove all the leading pathname components from a file name, leaving only the tail.

r   Remove a trailing suffix of the form *.xxx* from a file name, leaving the basename.

e Remove all but the trailing suffix from a file name.

For example,

```
%  history
50      cc -o image image.c fn1.c libim.a
51      image data1 data2 data3
52      lpr -v data3
53      lpr image.c
54      interpolate image1.im image2.im
55      image /usr/lib/images/moon.im
...
%  !cc:p
cc -o image image.c fn1.c libim.a
%  !!:s/fn1/fn2/
cc -o image image.c fn2.c libim.a
...output from compilation ...
%  echo !cc:$:r !int:2:r !int:2:e
echo libim image2 im
libim image2 im
%  echo !imag:1:h !imag:1:t
echo /usr/lib/images moon.im
/usr/lib/images moon.im
%
```

7.5 STANDARD INPUT AND OUTPUT

The commands for redirecting standard input and standard output are slightly different between the C-Shell and the Bourne shell; unfortunately, they are sufficiently similar as to be confusing. The basic redirection commands, ">", ">>" and "<" are precisely the same; the C-Shell provides the same technique as the Bourne shell for including the input to a command in a shell script using the command "<<" followed by a word which will be used to find the end of the input (see page 85).

The redirection of the standard error stream in C-Shell is quite different to the Bourne shell; whereas the Bourne shell uses the notation 2> to mean "re-direct file descriptor 2", the C-Shell uses the notation >& to mean "re-direct file descriptors 1 *and* 2" (standard output *and* standard error streams). If you wish to separate the output from file descriptors 1 and 2 into different files, the Bourne shell would require the command:

```
%   command > output 2> error
```

whereas the C-Shell would require the command:

```
%   (command > output) >& error
```

The C-Shell version will place the output from *command* into the file *output*; the output and error streams that are produced as a result will go into the file *error*.

The C-Shell provides the *noclobber* variable, which allows the user to avoid overwriting existing files; if *noclobber* is set, C-Shell will not allow the user to write to an existing file using the > redirection command; it will, however, allow the user to append to an existing file by using the >> redirection command.

7.6   FLOW OF CONTROL

Like the Bourne shell, the C-Shell includes many keyword constructs for loops and conditional execution.   The loop constructs are *foreach* and *while*.   The conditional statements are *if* and *switch*.

if makes use of the *exit status* of a command in the same way as the Bourne shell; unlike most versions of the Bourne shell, the C-Shell provides a number of built-in commands for testing various conditions such as the value of a variable or the status of file.

Expressions

The C-Shell provides a number of operators which can be used to combine and alter the values of variables. The most common operators are *comparison* operators which can be used to compare strings and numbers and *file inquiries* which can be used to test the status of a file or directory. Table 7.1 gives a list of comparison operators; table 7.2 gives a list of the common file inquiry operators.

Having looked at the structure of expressions, we can now return to the structure of control statements; the format of an *if* statement is either

```
if ( expression ) command
```

Comparison Operators	
Operator	**Result**
(...)	grouping
!	logical negation
<	less-than
>	greater-than
<=	less-than-or-equal-to
>=	greater-than-or-equal-to
&&	logical *and*
||	logical *or*

Table 7.1: Comparison Operators

File Inquiries	
Operator	**Result**
-r *file*	Returns true if you have read access.
-w *file*	True if you have write access.
-e *file*	True if the file exists.
-o *file*	True if you own the file.
-f *file*	True if *file* is a plain file.
-d *file*	True if *file* is a directory.
-z *file*	True if *file* is zero length.
-x *file*	True if *file* is executable.

Table 7.2: File Inquiries

or

```
if ( expression ) then
    command ...
else if ( expression 2 ) then
    ...
endif
```

If the *expression* is true, the first *command* is executed, and the rest skipped. If there is only one command after the *if*, the first form can be used; otherwise, the second form must be used. The *else* parts are optional. For example,

```
if ( -e $FILE )
then
      echo $FILE exists
else
      echo I have never heard of $FILE
endif
```

The other conditional statement is the *switch* statement; this provides a multi-way branch corresponding to the *case* statement in the Bourne shell. The format is

```
switch ( string )
      case label:
          ...
          breaksw
      default:
          ...
          breaksw
endsw
```

Each *label* is compared against the original *string* — if they are found to match, the statements following the *case* are executed. If none of the *labels* match, the *default* statements are executed. For example,

```
switch ($OPTION)
        case "-p":
        case "-P":
                print $FILE
                breaksw
        case "-[nN]":
                nroff $FILE
                breaksw
        default:
                echo unknown option $OPTION
                breaksw
endsw
```

Loops can be written using a *while* statement which repeatedly evaluates an expression, tests its exit status, and if it is true executes a sequence of commands; when the expression becomes false then C-Shell moves on to the statement following the loop. The format is

```
while ( expression )
do
        command sequence
        ...
end
```

For example

```
set reply=yes
while ( $reply == "yes" )
        echo "Here we go again\!"
        echo -n "Do you want to go again?"
        set reply=$<
end
```

There are two new features introduced in this example — the "$<" keyword which reads a string from the standard input and the *-n* option to the *echo* command which prevents *echo* from printing a newline character. The "$<" keyword is usually used, as in this example, to assign an input value to a variable.

The final looping construct is the *foreach* keyword, which takes the form

```
foreach variable ( word list )
        command sequence
end
```

The variable *var* is set to successive values of the *word list*; for each of
these values, the *command sequence* is executed. The command *continue*
can be used to continue the loop, skipping any remaining commands in
the sequence; the command *break* can be used to terminate the loop
before all the items in the *word list* have been processed. For example,

```
foreach file in (*)
        echo $file
        mv $file $file.old
end
```

7.7   STARTING THE SHELL FROM *login*

When you first login to Unix, you may find yourself in a C-Shell instead
of a Bourne shell — the choice is largely up to the person who manages
the system that you are using. When the C-Shell starts up, it first looks in
a file called *.cshrc* for commands and then, if this is a login shell, it looks
in a file called *.login.* This allows you to set up your own environment,
run any programs that you want, set certain variables, and so on. A typical
.cshrc might be

```
set path=($home/bin /etc /bin /usr/bin .)
# set the length of the history list
set history=30
# notify me about background tasks
set notify
# list my mail queue
if ($?prompt) from
```

The last line of this example makes use of the *prompt* variable to test
whether the shell is being run interactively. If a shell command is executed from within another program (for example, from within an editor
to obtain a list of files) the *.cshrc* file will be read when the C-Shell starts
up. However, you do not want the information that is printed by the *from*
command to appear in front of the list of files. By testing the *prompt*
variable, we can determine whether the shell is being run interactively
(in which case *prompt* is set) or in order to execute a shell script or batch
command (in which case *prompt* is not set and *from* will not be executed).

7.8   JOB CONTROL

The C-Shell takes advantage of an extended inter-process *signal* mechanism to allow you to manipulate several interactive jobs at once. At any one time, all but one of these jobs is either in the background, executing, or *stopped*, that is, suspended but ready to continue. The job which is currently in the foreground can be stopped by typing the *stop interrupt* key, which is normally ^Z on systems as distributed by Berkeley, but will be different on systems which use ^Z as end-of-file. The command *fg* can be used to bring a job into the foreground; *bg* resumes a currently stopped job in the background. *jobs* lists all current jobs.

When a background job requires terminal input, it will stop, and you will be notified by the C-Shell; when you are ready to provide the input, the job can be brought into the foreground. You have the choice of whether terminal output from background jobs should appear as it is produced, or be treated in the same way as input.

It is difficult to give the flavour of job control in a simple example, but part of a session might look like this (taking ^Z as the *stop* interrupt character):

```
%   cc -o myprog myprog.c
^Z
Stopped
%  bg
Push it into the background
[1] cc -o myprog myprog.c
%  ed newprog.c
2103
Editing session, interrupted by ...
[1] + Stopped (tty output) cc -o myprog myprog.c
^Z
Stopped
%  jobs
List current jobs
[1] + Stopped (tty output) cc -o myprog myprog.c
[2] - Stopped ed newprog.c
%  fg %1
Bring job 1 into the foreground
cc -o myprog myprog.c
"myprog.c", line 513:   syntax error
%   fg
ed newprog.c
```

`Continue editing session`

Useful as this facility is, some versions of Unix(such as SUNOS on Sun workstations and AUX on Apollo Domain workstations) go one better, and provide a *window manager*; the screen is divided into several, perhaps overlapping, areas, with a shell associated with each. Commands are available to change the window that is currently active, and to manipulate the position of the windows on the screen; these are often used with a mouse, graphics tablet, light pen, or similar "pointing" device. Such facilities are normally only available on systems with a high-resolution display, rather than a plain VDU terminal. For further discussion on this topic, see Section 13.4.

Chapter 8

More Commands

A particular strength of Unix is its wealth of software "tools"; the user has at her disposal a variety of utilities that other operating systems would make her write for herself. Here we shall list the most useful, together with some that may be considered essentials for any but the newest beginner. Like all Unix programs, they are invoked by giving their name to the shell as a command.

Each command has available *options* which will not be described exhaustively here; the manual will contain a full entry for each to use as reference. It is an unfortunate fact that specifying options to commands is not standardised under Unix; thus while it is usual (although not universal) for options to be preceded by a hyphen, or minus sign, "-", multiple options may require a hyphen each or may be juxtaposed. That is, we may need to supply options *a* and *b* thus

```
$   command -a -b [arguments]
```

and maybe thus

```
$   command -ab [arguments]
```

The on-line manual is the ultimate authority in this, and only experience will make you sure; be warned though that supplying options to a command in the wrong format may result in some of them being ignored.

Most commands will take arguments. Their nature — filename, character string, integer, ... — is usually clear from the context but most of the programs whose descriptions follow will take a file as input, either filter or process data from it, and produce output. It is the usual default that if the filename is not given explicitly *standard input* is read — likewise, output will be deposited on *standard output*.

8.1 *ar*

The concept of a *file archive* appears in at least two places in Unix, and you are quite likely to encounter both of them if you make more than casual use of a system. The first form is used in transporting files between Unix machines using the *tar* command — see page 162; the second form is created by the *ar* command, and is used extensively by the loader, *ld*, when you are compiling a program. The word *archive* is perhaps a misnomer in this context — it simply means that a number of files can be grouped together and referred to as a single file.

   ar is specifically designed for creating archives of partially-compiled object files, but there is no restriction on using *ar* to store other files. The Unix loader is able to read files created with *ar* and extract the component object files. To build an archive, you provide *ar* with the name of the archive and a list of files that are to be included in the archive; *ar* will create the archive file if it does not exist. *ar* has a variety of options for manipulating archives — *t* to display the contents of an archive, *x* to extract files from an archive, *d* to delete files from an archive and so on. For example, to compile a number of *C* functions and place them in an archive we would enter:

```
$  cc -c *.c
first.c:
second.c:
misc.c:
$  ar rv funcs.a first.o second.o misc.o
a - first.o
a - second.o
a - misc.o
ar:   creating funcs.a
```

To create an executable program that uses this archive, we could enter:

```
$  cc -o main main.c funcs.a
```

If, during the last stage, the compiler gives you an error message or a warning about the archive containing no "table of contents", you are probably using a Berkeley Unix system, and you should read about the command *ranlib* in the Unix manual; if, on the other hand, the compiler apparently fails to find some of the entries in the archive, you are probably using an AT&T version of Unix, and you need to read about the commands *lorder* and *tsort* for creating an ordered archive. The suffix that is used on the archive file — *.a* — is a Unix convention. Like so many Unix file naming conventions, it is primarily for your benefit rather than the benefit of the Unix software.

The archives that contain the standard library routines (those that appear in section 3 of the Unix manual) are stored in two main areas; the commonly-used routines and system calls are held in */lib/libc.a*, while the less frequently-used (and more esoteric) routines are held in a collection of libraries that match the pattern */usr/lib/lib*.a*.

8.2 *diff*

In Chapter 2 we met the command *cmp* to compare two files, and remarked that it did not report file differences in any detail; *diff* exists to do this. At its simplest, *diff* highlights the differences between two files by printing lines resembling *ed* commands that would bring the files into agreement, so

```
$  diff FILE1 FILE2
```

will search out the lines on which *FILE1* and *FILE2* differ. *diff* can do much better than this though; apart from options to elaborate on differences it can compare *directories* in the sense that it will run a standard *diff* comparison on files in different directories that share the same name, meanwhile reporting those file names that occur in but one of the specified directories. This unusual and powerful feature of a file comparison program makes handling of the Unix directory tree a much simpler task when multiple copies of files begin to cause clutter.

8.3 *find*

It is very common to be sure that a given file lies within a branch of the directory tree but not to know its precise home; *find* will search down the tree from a given point for a file (or files). The file may be specified in a variety of ways — by name, owner, protection, size, creation date, ...— or a combination of these.

find acts like a boolean operator, returning *true* or *false* for each file in the specified tree. A variety of options permit files satisfying the boolean condition to be submitted to other commands (a good example may be *rm*). An example of *find* in use is

```
$ find . -name "*.c" -print
./top.c
./alsotop.c
./dir1/onedown.c
./dir1/dir2/twodown.c
```

Here the search is conducted from the current directory, signified by "." hunting for files by name (the *-name* option). We search for all files whose name ends ".c" — notice that this specification is quoted to prevent the shell translating the asterisk; we want it passed to *find* literally. The action we specify is *-print* which will print all "true" files — that is, those matching the specification. What we see is the full pathname from the root we specified.

8.4   *grep*

A popular user requirement is to know whether a particular character string appears in a particular file, or group of files. It may be a search for a word in a textual document, for a variable name in a program or for any data item that can be described by a text string. *grep* (standing for General Regular Expression Parser, or possibly *g/RE/p* as an *ex* command, although *search* might have been a better name) provides this facility — we supply it with the string that interests us, the file(s) we wish to search, and it will display all lines that contain a match — thus to search *FILE* for the string *Shakespear* we say

```
$ grep Shakespear FILE
as Shakespear said in "Horse Trough", we
Shakespeare, though, is a different and
```

grep will print all lines in the file that include the specified string.

grep's power is extended by making the string specification accept various metacharacters (in particular all those understood by *ed*) and allowing the file specification to be as general as the shell permits; it is thus possible to search many files, or a complete directory at once. If more than one file is being searched, *grep* reports in which file it has found a match. For example

```
$ grep "^The H" *
elephants:The Howdah, pioneered by Esquimaux,
```

We have searched all files in the current directory for the string *"The H"* at the beginning of a line; it has been found precisely once in the file *elephants*.

8.5 *kill*

We have met the idea of creating independent processes in Chapters 5 and 6; frequently it is going to be necessary to exercise some control over them — perhaps to terminate them or otherwise interrupt them. *kill* allows *signals* to be sent to processes that the sender has the privilege to affect; all that is required is the process ID, which is available from the command *ps* (see below), or which is provided at startup for back-grounded processes. The command looks like

```
$ kill -n ID
```

where *n* and *ID* are both integers — the former the *signal* to send and the latter the process ID. The integer *n* is keyed to signals in the file */usr/include/signal.h*; it may translate to a number of things, for example "interrupt", "quit" or "kill" (with no questions asked). Some version of Unix, including Berkeley Unix, allow the signal number to be replaced by a signal *name*. Common signal names include *INT*, for interrupt, *HUP*, for hangup and *TERM* for terminate.

Signals are discussed further on page 141.

8.6 *mail*

Electronic mail is an oft-quoted benefit of multi-user computer systems. The Unix facility *mail* allows you to send mail to any other user on the system, whether she is logged in or not. At its simplest, use of *mail* looks like

```
$ mail jim
This is the text of the message
```

User *jim* would receive the message as typed; when he next logged in he would be alerted by the message

```
You have mail
```

appearing on his screen.

Mail is read by giving the *mail* command with no arguments; the latest message to be received will be displayed. After this a number of commands are available, specifically reading other messages, message deleting (*d*) and on-line help (*?*). For instance, *jim* at his next login may type

```
$  mail
From ufu Mon Jul 18 20:10:54 1983
To:  jim

This is the text of the message

d
ⓔ
$
```

mail comes in many versions; for full details of your local flavour see the manual, but this description has only scratched the surface of its capabilities whatever features your particular version may offer. The issues involved in electronic mail are discussed further on page 205 in the chapter on Communications.

8.7   *od*

While you are a novice user, you will read some files and execute others. The day will come, however, when it will be necessary to interrogate the contents of a "binary" file — a file that is raw (unreadable) data, an executable program or anything that may contain unprintable characters. The utility *od* will do this; by default it decodes sixteen bit words into octal, but options exist to decode eight bit bytes, attempt translation to ASCII and alter the output radix. For example

```
$  od FILE
```

would print on the terminal the octal contents of *FILE* interpreted as a stream of sixteen bit words, while

```
$  od -bc FILE
```

would do the same for eight bit bytes (via the *b* option), while trying to interpret them as ASCII characters (the *c* option).

8.8 *pr*

Whatever the convenience of video terminals, the time comes when hard copy is essential; the utility *pr* acts as a filter to prepare a file for listing on a lineprinter or hard copy device. What this device may be, of course, is site dependent; the usual use of *pr* is to pipe its output into a spooler, if one exists locally, or to write it to a hard copy terminal. Whichever, *pr* is capable of page numbering, sending form feeds to square output on the page, multi-column output and various other features; in particular, each page will be headed by the file's name and the date of printing, although options exist to control this header. A simple example that would produce two column output on the standard output channel is

```
$  pr -2 FILE
```

8.9 *ps*

A particular power of Unix is its ability to run several processes for you at once; a corollary to this power is a requirement for information on how such processes may be faring. *ps*, with no arguments, will report on all the calling user's current processes giving their unique process number, consumption of CPU, time and memory, running status and the command that initiated them.

Various arguments make *ps* a powerful tool for examining all processes on the system, making interrogation of non-interactive jobs (for example, spoolers) possible. A lengthy manual entry provides a good education.

8.10   *sleep*

As your use of Unix grows more sophisticated, uses for delaying a command's execution may occur. The command *sleep*, followed by an integer argument, accomplishes this; so

```
$   sleep 10
```

would cause the shell to slumber for 10 seconds. It is not of much value thus baldly used — it would normally be combined with another command, something like

```
$   (sleep 10; echo "10 seconds have expired")&
```

In this manner a command would be executed after a chosen delay as a background process.

sleep finds many uses in shell scripts.

8.11   *sort*

Every operating system will include a utility to sort files; such sorting may usually be done on a numerical or alphabetical basis, in ascending or descending order, with respect to specific characters in a line, with any number of other possible frills. Unix provides *sort* which also offers every complication you could ever ask for.

A pleasant feature of *sort* is its assumption that generally sorting is going to be a straightforward alphabetic business, so

```
$   sort FILE > FILE.sorted
```

will sort the lines in *FILE* into alphabetical order, and write them into *FILE.sorted*. For a full exposition on the power of *sort*, which is considerable, consult the manual. Suffice it to say that the options are many and that most reasonable sorts may be accomplished using it.

8.12   *stty*

The terminal you work at has a number of characteristics, some obvious and some transparent, with which Unix will communicate to assist you.

It will know, for instance, that the TAB character is really an instruction to move to the next multiple-of-eight position on a line; also various characters are available to perform rubouts, or line deletes during input. The command *stty* will list these for you, and permit you to change them.

```
$  stty
```

will list all principal features of the terminal. Each of these features may be toggled or changed by giving *stty* the correct argument — thus

```
$  stty -echo
```

will turn off computer echo at your terminal, while

```
$  stty echo
```

will turn it on.

Many versions of Unix provide an option to *stty* to reset the terminal to a known, sensible, state. Often it is

```
$  stty sane
```

but it may be

```
$  reset
```

stty varies from implementation to implementation; there will probably be an option available to list *all* the terminal features that it understands. The manual will contain a comprehensive list of terminal parameters, together with their meanings.

8.13 *tail*

It is always easy to inspect the top of a file simply by typing it out; frequently we will do this and abort the typing as soon as we have seen whatever interests us pass by. Unix provides *tail* to inspect the *end* of a file in the same manner

```
$  tail FILE
```

will type the last ten lines of *FILE*,

```
$  tail +N FILE
```

produces lines from *N* to the end, while

```
$  tail -N FILE
```

will give the last *N* lines. Due to limited buffer space in *tail*, there is a finite limit on the amount of information that you can ask for relative to the end of a file.

8.14   *tee*

The filter *tee* does nothing to its standard input save write it to its standard output; it does however take a filename as argument into which it puts a copy of standard input. As its name suggests, it is used as a T-junction on pipelines to take a copy of an intermediate product of a composite command. Thus

```
$  diff FILE1 FILE2 | tee FILE.diff | grep insidious
```

will print on standard output differences between *FILE1* and *FILE2* that include the word "insidious" — all differences, though, will be recorded in *FILE.diff*

8.15   *tr*

Frequently files require a global alteration of a simple kind — perhaps one character needs translating to another. A common example is changing a character that is unavailable on a local printer to something analogous that is available. The filter program *tr* performs such translation; if we wanted to substitute all occurrences of braces "{}" in *FILE* by parentheses "()" for instance, we could say

```
$  tr "{}" "()" < FILE > FILE.fixed
```

Note that *tr* takes two strings as arguments. The strings should be of equal length, then substitution of characters in corresponding positions is done. If the second string is shorter than the first, it is padded by repeating its last character. Note also that *tr* reads only standard input (in this example redirected from *FILE*).

tr has options that permit quite sophisticated manipulation of files beyond simple translation — consult the manual before using it.

8.16 *wc*

ls with its *-l* option will provide the size of a file in bytes; very often for text files it is useful to know how those bytes are allocated to words and lines, and the word counting program *wc* does this.

```
$ wc FILE
400 2482 14651
```

wc tells us that *FILE* contains 400 lines, 2482 words and 14651 characters. The line and word data are necessarily approximate, but *words* are deemed to be separated by spaces, tabs or newline characters, and *lines* by newline characters. *wc* is thus bound to get a little confused by files containing overprinting or underlining but it is of great value as a document yardstick.

8.17 *write*

If you are sure that a user you wish to contact is logged on, *write* provides a quicker communication than *mail*. Its action is to open the destination user's terminal and deposit on it lines typed at your own; for example

```
$ write jim
Herewith an instant message
```

write will of course report if it cannot find the specified user logged on; another possible failure message is

```
write: Permission denied
```

indicating that the proposed recipient has turned off permission to write to his terminal by using the command *mesg*. You may do this yourself:

```
$   mesg n
```

will prevent intrusive messages arriving; an argument *y* instead of *n* will re-permit them. *mesg* without arguments provides the current write status of your terminal.

8.18   *talk*

Some Unix systems provide the *talk* command as an alternative to the *write* command — *talk* allows a split-screen conversation between two users, possibly between separate machines. When a user issues a *talk* request by entering a command such as

```
$   talk mdt@olympus
```

the *talk* command will notify the user "mdt" on the remote Unix system called "olympus" that someone is trying to talk to her; if she responds with a matching *talk* command, a two-way conversation is set up between the two users.

Some Unix systems provide the *phone* command which allows a multi-way conversation — users can "join in" a *phone* session, and each users' screen displays what the other users are typing. While *talk* provides a simple two-way conversation, *phone* is, in essence, a primitive conferencing facility.

The protocols underlying *talk* and *phone* are discussed in Chapter 13.

Chapter 9

C and the Unix Interface

C is the most widely available programming language on Unix; this is hardly surprising, since most of the Unix system and its utilities are themselves written in C, which was itself designed by Dennis Ritchie, one of the principal architects of Unix. The language is described in detail in the book *The C Programming Language* [9]; the first edition of this book describes the language that was used to implement most current versions of Unix; the second (and current) edition describes the language that is likely to be accepted as an ANSI standard. We do not intend to describe it here owing to lack of space. We shall therefore assume that you have acquired some familiarity with C, although you will not need to be fluent in the more advanced aspects of the language.

The C compiler is invoked on most Unix systems by the command *cc*, which has many options. By default, the executable file produced by *cc* is called *a.out*, so that you can compile and run a C program by entering

```
$  cc myprog.c
$  a.out
```

The option "-o *name*" puts the executable file in *name*:

```
$  cc -o myprog myprog.c
$  myprog
```

A program can be composed of several files, which can be compiled together by

```
$  cc -o bigprog mainpart.c subpart1.c subpart2.c
mainpart.c:
subpart1.c:
subpart2.c:
```

127

You should refer to the Programmer's Manual for full details of other options.

C communicates with Unix through a library of functions which invoke services called *system calls*. Just as we said in Chapter 1 that there is in a sense in which the kernel is the part of the system which truly defines Unix, so the collection of available system calls completely defines the behaviour of the kernel as far as the user is concerned. Every Unix system call is accessible to the C programmer. They are catalogued and described in Section 2 of the Programmer's Manual; we shall not reproduce here the detail available there, but will give a brief description of each call and its use. This is probably the driest section of the entire book; however, the system calls are the heart of Unix, and we make no apology for devoting so much space to them.

In addition to the system calls, a number of higher-level library functions are available to the C programmer. Some of these are entirely specific to Unix, while others are not, and are available in many implementations of C on other operating systems. The latter constitute the C *standard library*. Those library functions that are not system calls are described in Section 3 of the Programmer's Manual. We shall describe only those of them which relate particularly to Unix, although a complete list can be found in Appendix 2.

Following the distinction we have just drawn, we shall divide this chapter into three sections: System Calls, Unix-Specific Library Functions, and a final section on program development aids on Unix. You should bear in mind whilst reading this chapter that the boundary between system calls and library routines is largely dependent upon each implementation of Unix — some of the calls that are classed here as system calls may well be library routines on some versions of Unix, and *vice versa*.

9.1   A NOTE ON *ANSI* C

The American National Standards Committee is slowly moving towards creating a standard version of C, which differs slightly from the C used in this chapter. The main difference between the language defined in [9] and the draft standard descibed in [10] is in the definition of functions. In "old" C, a function might be declared as follows:

```
func(ix, jx)
        int ix, jx;
{
        ...
```

in ANSI C, this function would be declared as follows:

```
int func(int ix, int jx)
{
        ...
```

ANSI C also allows stricter type-checking by the use of *function prototypes*; in old C, a function that is declared in one file (say x.c) can be referred to in another file (say y.c) without the types of the arguments to the function being specified in file y.c. In ANSI C, a *function prototype* can be inserted in the file y.c, thus allowing the compiler to check the types of the arguments to the function. A function prototype for the function declared above would be

```
int func(int, int);
```

Notice that the argument names are not given — only the argument *types* are specified.

Although ANSI C compilers are becoming more popular and available, it should be pointed out that [10] is a draft standard; since the majority of C compilers are still "old" C, the function descriptions in this chapter are given in old C syntax.

9.2   A WARNING ON POINTERS IN C

Before describing the libraries, a word of caution is needed, owing to an unfortunate ambiguity in the Programmer's Manual. Consider, for example, the synopsis in the manual of the routine *stat*:

```
stat(name, buf)
        char    *name;
        struct  stat *buf;
```

stat obtains information about a file and returns it in the structure *buf*. Many beginners (and others), on reading this entry, write a piece of code such as

```
report (filename)
        char *filename
{
        struct    stat *buf;
        if (stat(filename, buf) == -1)
                ...
```

This code is a program error, and the most probable consequence of running it is a core dump. (A *core dump* is a file called *core* in the current directory which contains a binary image of the state of a program upon termination; it can be examined using a program such as *adb* or *dbx* to investigate the cause of error). The problem is that although *stat* requires an object of type "pointer to *buf* structure" as argument, it is necessary that the programmer should set up the pointer beforehand so that it really does point to some valid structure. The above declaration does not do this; it declares an uninitialised pointer, which does not yet point to anything meaningful. There are at least two reasonable idioms that can be used to achieve the desired result (most programmers seem to use the former):

```
report (filename)
        char       *filename
{
        struct    stat buf;
        if (stat(filename, &buf) == -1)
                ...
```
or
```
report (filename)
        char       *filename
{
        struct    stat buf[1];
        if (stat(filename, buf) == --1)
                ...
```

In general, whenever a system call requires a pointer argument which is to be set to point to data returned by the call, it is the responsibility of the programmer to make sure that the pointer refers to a valid object.

9.3   SYSTEM CALLS

Most system calls can potentially return an error result, which is usually an integer with the value -1. When a call results in an error, the variable *errno* (which needs to be declared as *extern int*), contains an error code explaining the error; error codes are listed in the introduction to Section 2 of the manual.

The calls described in this section are those that are common to the Berkeley Standard Distribution (**BSD**) of Unix and the AT&T System V.3 version of Unix. Many of these system calls have been inherited from Version 7 of Unix, but many of them are only relevant to the more recent versions of the system. Other systems differ slightly in some calls, and many provide extra facilities; you should consult your Programmer's Manual for details. Most of the system calls are described in this chapter, but we omit details of some of the more obscure or esoteric ones, normally of interest only to the advanced system programmer. For convenience of organisation, we divide system calls into four categories: those pertaining to files and I/O, to process creation and manipulation, to timing and related services, and miscellaneous others. Within these headings, we have tried to group related calls together as far as possible, and to follow a progression from most commonplace to most obscure. (Appendix 2 lists system calls and other functions alphabetically). Types left unspecified below are all *int*. Many calls require the inclusion of *header files* to define appropriate structures; see the Programmer's Manual for these.

Files and I/O

```
open(path, flags, mode)
        char    *path;
        int     flags;
        int     mode;
```

open returns an integer which can be used by various system calls, such as *read* and *write*, to access the file whose name is the string passed as the argument *path*. *flags* specifies whether the file is to be opened for reading (*flags* = 0), writing (1), or both (2). *flags* can be logically or'ed with other constants (using the "|" operator in *C*) to produce effects such as creating the file or opening at the end of the file. Many systems will provide a header file giving symbolic names to these flag constants, such as *O_RDONLY* for *flags* = 0. If the file is created by the *open* call, *mode* specifies the *access modes* of the file after creation — it is usually given as an octal constant. The mode may also be modified by *umask*, described on page 140. The integer returned by *open* is known as a *file descriptor*. Three file descriptors are normally open when a process is started: the standard input is open as descriptor 0, the standard output as 1, and the standard error as 2.

```
close(filedescriptor)
        int     filedescriptor;
```

The open file with the given *filedescriptor* is closed; that is, subsequent system calls using that descriptor become invalid. All open files are closed when a program finishes; however, it is good programming practice to close a file as soon as you have finished with it, since Unix limits the number of files a program may have open at once.

```
creat(filename, mode)
        char    *filename;
        int     mode;
```

The named file is created if it did not exist before, otherwise made empty; if it is newly created, the mode is set to the given value, as described under *chmod* in Chapter 4 (the mode may be modified by *umask*, described on page 140). (You should bear in mind that library functions and commands may have the same names — this can be confusing, particularly when you are searching the index of the Unix Programmer's Manual.) *creat* opens the file for writing, and returns a suitable file descriptor. It has largely been made obsolete by the *open* system call described above.

```
read(filedescriptor, buffer, nbytes)
        int     filedescriptor;
        char    *buffer;
        int     nbytes;
```

Up to *nbytes* characters are read in from the file whose descriptor is given, and placed in the area pointed to by *buffer*. The number of characters actually read is returned as the result of *read*; if end-of-file has been reached, the call will return 0; in the event of an error, it will return −1. The return value may be less than *nbytes*; for example, if the file is a terminal, *read* will usually never read in more than a single line of input at a time.

```
write(filedescriptor, buffer, nbytes)
        int     filedescriptor;
        char    *buffer;
        int     nbytes;
```

Up to *nbytes* characters are copied from the area pointed to by *buffer* to the file whose descriptor is given. The number of characters actually written out is returned as the result of *write*.

```
long lseek(filedescriptor, offset, wherefrom)
        int         filedescriptor;
        off_t       offset;
        int         wherefrom;
```

The next access to the file (open for reading or writing) will be at a location defined by *offset* [1] and *wherefrom*:

Wherefrom	Next Access At
0	*offset* bytes from start
1	*offset* bytes from current position
2	*offset* bytes after the current end-of-file

In the last case, *offset* is more often than not zero or negative, allowing the programmer to find a location near end-of-file very quickly. *lseek* returns the offset from the beginning of the file of the next access. Hence *lseek(f, (off_t) 0, 1)* returns the current position.

```
dup(olddescriptor)
        int         olddescriptor;
dup2(olddescriptor1, newdescriptor2)
        int         olddescriptor1,
                    newdescriptor2;
```

dup returns another descriptor synonymous with the given one. That is, *reads* and *writes* on the new descriptor will refer to the same file, and the current position in the file of the two descriptors will always remain in step. In practice, the result of *dup* is always the least currently unused descriptor, so that many system programs contain fragments similar to:

```
close(0);       /* close standard input */
dup(fd);        /* make fd the new standard input */
close(fd);      /* and release the file descriptor */
```

which allows all future references to the standard input (always file descriptor 0) to refer to the file attached to *fd*. However, rather than rely on this, *dup2* can be used; this explicitly asks for the second descriptor to be made synonymous with the first, after being closed if it refers to a currently open file, so that

```
dup2(fd, 0);
close(fd);
```

would be equivalent to the earlier example that makes use of *dup*.

```
pipe(descriptorpair)
        int         descriptorpair[2];
```

---

[1]The type of *offset*, *off_t*, is usually defined in a system header file such as *types.h*; it is quite often a synonym for a long integer.

pipe creates a channel for inter-process communication.   *descriptor-pair[0]* becomes a descriptor open for reading and *descriptorpair[1]* for writing, on an anonymous "file" called a "pipe". When a process with an open pipe *forks* (see next section), both the resulting processes have access to the pipe. Hence they can communicate with each other; one process writes on the pipe while the other reads from it. This is the mechanism used to implement pipelines in the shell, and is common mechanism used to implement inter-process communication between processes that have a parent in common. If two processes do not have a parent in common, inter-process communication is a little more difficult — see Chapter 13.

```
link(oldname, newname)
        char     *oldname;
        char     *newname;
```

A file whose name is given as *newname* is created as a link to the existing file *oldname*, i.e. the two names become synonyms for the same file; cf. the *ln* command described in Chapter 4. It is a feature of most versions of Unix that both file names must lie in the same file system.

```
unlink(filename)
        char     *filename;
```

The name given as *filename* is removed from its directory. However, the corresponding file is not actually deleted until there are no links to it, and no open file descriptor referring to it.

```
chmod(filename, mode)
        char     *filename;
        int      mode;
```

The mode of *filename* is set to the given *mode*, which is usually given in octal. The low-order 9 bits of *mode* specify read/write/execute permission for the owner of the file, for those in the same group as the owner, and others. The next 3 bits specify respectively "set user ID on execution", "set group ID on execution", and "sticky text segment". The first two of these are discussed in the next section, under the system calls *getuid* and *getgid*.   The third is an efficiency measure designed to ensure that programs which are frequently run, but which are not running [2] constantly, can be loaded more quickly into memory when required. The use of the "sticky bit" has largely been superseded in recent versions of Unix by a variety of features, such as efficient virtual memory manage-

---

[2] e.g. programs such as *ed* and the C compiler routines, but *not* the shell.

ment and, most recently, by the dynamic linking of functions into running programs.

```
chown(filename, owner, group)
        char    *filename;
        int     owner,
                group;
```

In most versions of Unix, this is available only to the super-user; it resets the owner and group of *filename*. On Berkeley versions of Unix, a user can be in a number of groups simultaneously — a programmer may use the *chown* call to change the group of a file to any one of the groups that the owner of the file belongs to.

```
stat(filename, buffer)
        char    *filename;
        struct  stat *buffer;
```

```
fstat(filedescriptor, buffer)
        int     filedescriptor;
        struct  stat *buffer;
```

stat and *fstat* obtain information about a file, placing it in *buffer*; the information includes filetype, protection, owner, and times of creation, last change, and last access. The precise contents of *buffer* may vary considerably from one version of Unix to another. *stat* returns information about the file whose name is passed as first argument, whereas *fstat* requires instead a descriptor for a currently open file as first argument.

```
ioctl (filedescriptor, request, buffer)
        int     filedescriptor;
        int     request;
        char    *buffer;
```

ioctl is a very general system call that allows the programmer to examine and change the attributes of character special (or *raw*) input/output devices; the list of operations that are available on a given *filedescriptor* will depend heavily on the device to which it refers. For example, devices such as magnetic tape drives may allow the programmer to skip forward and backward over blocks; devices such as disk controllers may allow the superuser to issue formatting requests and to query the bad block list. The most common use of *ioctl* is to control the attributes of a users terminal. In AT&T System V, the data structure and the *ioctl* calls to control terminal devices are documented under *termio*. Common BSD *ioctl* requests are *TIOCGETP* (return status information in *buffer*) and *TIOCSETP* (set status information according to the contents of *buffer*). Most commonly, the TIOCGETP and TIOCSETP requests are used to obtain and alter the attributes of a terminal, such as line speed, whether characters are to be echoed, and whether the terminal is an uppercase-only device. The use of *ioctl* on different devices is described in the entry for the corresponding device in section 4 of the Programmer's Manual.

```
access(filename, mode)
        char     *filename;
        int      mode;
```

access is used by certain privileged programs to discover whether the user running the program has permission to access the file in the way specified by *mode*, which is a 3-bit octal number — 4=*read*, 2=*write*, 1=*execute*, as in *chmod*. A *mode* of 0 will simply test whether the file exists or not, and is accessible to the programmer in any way.

```
mknod(filename, mode, device)
        char     *filename;
        int      mode;
        int      device;
```

mknod creates a *special file*, or a named pipe (or *FIFO*), described in Chapter 13; under AT&T System V, it can also create a directory, whereas Berkeley Unix provides a *mkdir* system call to create directories. Normally, only the super-user can create special files such as character special devices, block special devices or directories; ordinary users can create *FIFO*'s. Under Berkeley Unix, ordinary users can use the *mkdir* system call to create directories. Under AT&T Unix, only the super-user can create directories using *mknod*; if a programmer wishes to create a directory under AT&T Unix, she will usually use the *system* function to call the *mkdir* program.

```
utimes(filename, times)
        char     *filename;
        time_t   times[2];
```

utime sets the time of last access and last update on a file to the times given in *times*. It is primarily useful for archive programs such as *tar*.

Process Creation and Manipulation

A *process* is in essence a single running program; it may be a "system" program, such as *login*, *update*, or *sh*, or a user program. A few programs run as several separate communicating processes. A process is created by the *fork* system call, described in this section. *fork* turns a single process into two identical processes, known as the *parent* and the *child*. Processes thus have an ancestry of parent, grandparent, and so on, all the way back to *init*, which is the progenitor of them all. The system calls in this section are used to discover or change features of the process making them, or to communicate with other processes.

```
exit (status)
        int        status;
_exit (status)
        int        status;
```

exit terminates the process which calls it, returning the value of *status* as its *exit status*. By convention, a *status* of 0 means "normal termination", and any other value indicates an error or unusual occurrence. When a process exits, all its open files are closed, after completion of any pending I/O operations. The call _*exit(status)*; causes immediate termination without attempting to clean up; this can be useful in child processes in the event of an *exec* call failing.

```
fork ()
vfork ()
```

The process calling *fork* splits into two identical processes; the only difference is that in the *parent* process, the call returns a number called the *process ID* of the child (which is always non-zero), whereas in the child it returns 0. The process which called *fork* is always the parent. A common idiom for process creation is

```
int processid;
switch (processid=fork())
{
        case -1:
                /* Fork failed:   report error */
                break;
        case 0:
                /* This is the child;
                   act appropriately */
                break;
        default:
                /* This is the parent;
                   act appropriately */
                break;
}
```

fork is almost always followed in the child process immediately by a call of one of the flavours of *exec*. The *vfork* system call is available on Berkeley versions of Unix; it is designed to allow the programmer to *fork* very large processes efficiently, although it is rapidly becoming obsolete with advances in virtual memory techniques and copy-on-write strategies.

```
execl(filename, arg0, arg1,..., argn, (char *)0)
        char    *filename;
        char    *arg0, *arg1,..., *argn;
execv(filename, argv)
        char    *filename;
        char    *argv[];
execle(filename, arg0, arg1,..., argn, (char *)0, env)
        char    *filename;
        char    *arg0, *arg1,..., *argn, *env[];
execve(filename, argv, env)
        char    *filename, *argv[], *env[];
```

All these calls replace the program in the current process by the one stored in *filename*; the new program is started, retaining the former process ID, in place of the calling program. All open file descriptors remain valid in the new process; in particular, standard input (descriptor 0), output (1) and error (2) are inherited by the new program. When a program starts, it is passed a vector of strings as argument; this can be specified either as an argument-list, terminated by a NULL pointer, to *execl*, or as a vector, with last element 0, to *execv*. The process *environment* can be specified explicitly as a vector of strings *env* to either *execle* or *execve*. The environment is, in essence, a list of variable names with associated string values, and is typically inherited from the shell as a list of its *exported* variables. *execl* and *execv* pass the environment of the calling program to the new one.

In a C program, the argument vector and environment vector are available as arguments of the start-up function *main*, which receives three arguments altogether — those just mentioned, together with a count of the number of arguments:

```
main(argcount, argvector, envvector)
        int     argcount;
        char    *argvector[];
        char    *envvector[];
```

although most programs ignore the third argument, and access their environment through the higher-level function *getenv*.

A program started from the shell receives the user's command-line arguments as the argument vector to *main*. By convention, it is usual to arrange in the *exec* call that *argvector[0]* is set to the name of the program to be executed, e.g.

```
execl("/bin/ed", "ed", "myfile", (char *)0);
```

which corresponds to the shell command

```
$ ed myfile
```

You normally need to specify a full pathname for programs to be *exec* ed; two further forms, however, are *execlp* and *execvp*, which search for *filename* in each directory on your *PATH*.

```
wait(status)
        int     *status;
```

This is used by a parent process; the process becomes dormant in the *wait* routine until one of its children exits, whereupon it returns from *wait* and wakes up. The process ID of the terminated process is returned as the result of *wait*, and its exit status is put into the word pointed to by *status*, together with further flags to indicate whether the process exited normally, or failed with an error (and possibly a core-dump).

Berkeley Unix provides a more sophisticated version of the *wait* call.

```
wait(status)
        union   wait    *status;
wait3(status, options, rusage)
        union   wait    *status;
        int     options;
        struct  rusage  *rusage;
```

The Berkeley versions of *wait* provide more detailed status information about the child process when it terminates.

It is inconvenient that *wait* is not selective; to wait for a particular child to finish, something like the following is needed:

```
wait_for (pid)
int     pid;
{
        int     status[1];
        int     justdied;
        while ((justdied=wait(status)) != pid)
                if (justdied == -1)
                        error();
                        /* no more children alive */
        .../* Carry on */

}
```

```
    getpid()
```
getpid returns the process ID of the process which called it.
```
    chdir(filename)
            char      *filename;
```
filename is made the current directory for the calling process; all sub-sequent pathnames not starting with a "/" are relative to this directory.

```
    chroot(filename)
            char      *filename;
```
filename becomes the root directory of the file system for the calling process. This call is restricted to the super-user.
```
    umask(mode)
            int       mode;
```
The protection mode on all files subsequently created by this process will be modified by setting to 0 all those bits which are set to 1 in mode; *cf.* the *umask* command described in Chapter 4. For example, a mode of 07 will ensure that all files are created unreadable, unwriteable and unexecutable by anyone other than the owner and those in her group.
```
    getuid()
    geteuid()
    getgid()
    getegid()
```
Every process on Unix has associated with it a *real* and *effective* user ID and group ID. The effective IDs determine what access permissions the process has; that is, they are compared with the *owner* and *group* fields of a file's protection to see which set of permissions to use. The real IDs identify under what username and group the user who started the process logged in. It is possible for the real and effective user IDs to be different, because some programs can set either or both of user or group ID to those of the owner and group of the file. This makes it possible to write a program which any user can run, which can access sensitive data to which she does not normally have access. For example, it would clearly be unsafe to let all users have write permission on the system password file, yet to change her password a user needs to be able to amend this file. Hence the system program *passwd* runs with its effective user ID set to that of the owner of the password file, so that a user running it *can* alter the file, but only in ways allowed by *passwd*.

   getuid and *getgid* return the real user and group IDs; *geteuid* and *getegid* return the effective IDs.

```
setuid(userid)
        int        userid;
setgid(groupid)
        int        groupid;
seteuid(userid)
        int        userid;
setegid(groupid)
        int        groupid;
```

These calls set both real and effective user or group ID to that given as argument; ordinary mortals are allowed these calls only if the argument is their *real* user or group ID, but a process running as super-user can set the IDs to anything. These calls are used, for example, by *login*, which runs as super-user until a user has completed a successful login, whereupon *login* sets its user and group IDs to those of the user and *exec*s a shell. The *setuid* and *setgid* calls set both the real and effective user (and group) id's. The *seteuid* and *setegid* calls are available on Berkeley Unix — they allow the programmer to set the effective user and group id's independently of the real user and group id's.

```
kill(processid, signalnumber)
        int        processid;
        int        signalnumber;
```

kill sends a *signal* to the process whose ID is given as argument. The usual default action taken by a process on receiving a signal is to terminate execution, usually with a core dump, but a process may define routines which are called whenever a particular signal is received, or may ignore a signal altogether. The only exception is the signal *SIGKILL*, which terminates the receiving process unconditionally, provided that the sender and receiver have the same effective user ID. *Cf.* the *kill* command in Chapter 8.

```
int (*signal(signalnumber, action))()
        int        signalnumber;
        int        (*action)();
```

This incomprehensible-looking declaration means that *signal* takes as its second argument a pointer to a function, and returns a pointer to a function as result. The *action* specified is called when next the specified *signalnumber* is received; if *action* is *SIGIGN*, all future occurrences of the signal are ignored, while if it is *SIGDFL* the standard default handling of it is restored.

Signals occur in one of three ways:

1. Because a process has explicitly sent one, using the *kill* system call; any signal at all can be sent in this way.

2. Because the kernel has sent one. Examples include the *SIGINT* and *SIGQUIT* signals, delivered in response to the user typing the interrupt and quit characters on her keyboard, and the *SIGALRM* signal, which is sent in response to an *alarm* system call, described in the next section.

3. Because some internal condition, usually erroneous, has arisen. Examples include floating point overflow, attempt to access a memory address not available to the process or to execute an invalid or privileged hardware instruction, and writing on a pipe when there is no process there to read from it.

Under Berkeley Unix and System V there are a number of differences in the way in which signals are handled. Under Berkeley Unix, when a signal is received the following events occur:

1. the interrupt service routine is called; while the interrupt service routine is executing, any further instances of the same signal are blocked until the service routine is finished.

2. when the service routine is finished, the signal handler is retained automatically — any further instances of the same signal will trap to the same service routine.

Under System V, signal handling is somewhat different. When a signal is received, the signal handler that will be called when the *next* instance of this signal is received is reset to the default handler; the signal handler is then invoked. For some signals, this implies that any future signal of this type will be ignored; for other signal types, the program will terminate with a core dump. It is therefore quite important under System V to reinstall the signal handler as soon as you enter the service routine if you wish further signals to be caught.

For example, the following code will trap the user typing INTER-RUPT, set a flag to indicate that the interrupt has to be dealt with and continue execution each time. (Under Berkeley Unix, the first line of the *wheninterrupted* function would not be necessary — however, it will do no harm.)

```
wheninterrupted()
{
        signal(SIGINT, wheninterrupted);
        service_interrupt = 1;
        return;
        /* Resume processing at the point
         * where the interrupt was received
         */
}

main()
{
        int     wheninterrupted();
        signal(SIGINT, wheninterrupted);
        ...
```

Under Berkeley Unix, *signal* is implemented using the lower-level system call *sigvec* — the *signal* interface is retained, and it behaves in a very similar manner to the *signal* call of System V. The *sigvec* system call gives the programmer a slightly finer degree of control over signal handling and avoids problems with rapidly repeated signals, but most applications will find *signal* quite adequate.

```
nice(increment)
        int     increment;
```

The priority of the calling process has *increment* added. If *increment* is positive, the effect is to give the process less of the machine's attention; conversely, if negative (allowed only for the super-user), the process is given preferential treatment.

```
caddr_t brk(address)
        caddr_t address;
caddr_t sbrk(increment)
        int     increment;
```

These are the low-level routines used to obtain extra memory for a process and subsequently relinquish it. The C programmer will usually, however, use higher-level space managements functions such as *malloc* or *calloc* and *free*. The *caddr_t* type will be system-dependent — it will usually be declared in a header file to be *char* * on pre-ANSI compilers, and *void* * on ANSI compilers.

```
profil(buffer, buffersize, offset, scale)
        char    *buffer;
        int     buffersize;
        int     offset;
        int     scale;
```

profil can be used to gather execution statistics for a program. It is rarely used directly by user programs, but provides the basis of the execution profile analysed by the program *prof*.

```
ptrace(request, processid, address, data)
        int     request;
        int     processid;
        char    *address;
        int     data;
```

ptrace allows one process to control the execution of another. It is used by debuggers such as *adb*, but rarely if ever by normal users.

Timing Services

```
time_t time(timelocation)
        long    *timelocation;
ftime(timebuffer)
        struct  timeb *timebuffer;
gettimeofday(tp, tzp)
        struct  timeval *tp;
        struct  timezone *tzp;
```

time returns the number of seconds since 00:00:00 GMT, Jan. 1st, 1970. If *timelocation* is non-zero, then the same value is also put into **timeloca-tion.* Berkeley Unix provides the *ftime* and *gettimeofday* calls which provide more detail than the *time* call, including distance from Greenwich, whether Daylight Saving Time is in force and the time to the nearest millisecond; this accuracy may be spurious, since many Unix systems have clocks which are accurate only to the nearest 50th or 60th of a second.

```
stime(timelocation)
        long    *timelocation;
```

stime resets the system clock to the value pointed to by *timelocation* (seconds since 00:00:00 GMT, Jan. 1, 1970). This is permitted only to the super-user.

```
times(timesbuffer)
        struct  tbuffer *timesbuffer;
```

times reports CPU time used by this process and those of its descendants which have terminated, divided into *user* time and *system* time; the latter is in effect the time Unix has used in servicing the process' system calls. This call is obsolete in later versions of Berkeley Unix which provide the

```
getrusage(who, rusage)
        int     who;
        struct  rusage  *rusage;
```

function which provides detailed timing and resource information about a process, or about the children of a process.

```
alarm(nseconds)
        unsigned nseconds;
```

```
getitimer(which, value)
        int     which;
        struct  itimerval *value;
setitimer(which, value, oldvalue);
        int     which;
        struct  itimerval *value;
        struct  itimerval *oldvalue;
```

alarm requests that a *SIGALRM* signal be sent to the calling process after *nseconds* seconds have elapsed. If *nseconds* is zero, any pending alarm request is cancelled. Berkeley Unix gives the programmer a wider range of timing facilities in the form of the *getitimer* and *setitimer* system calls — under Berkeley Unix, each process is provided with three interval timers counting in real time, virtual time (which exists only when a process is running) and profile time (which exists when the process is running, or when the system is executing a system call for the process); each timer ticks at the resolution of the machine's clock.

```
pause()
```

pause causes the calling process to suspend execution; it is used by processes which wish to do nothing until an external signal (from another process, or in response to an *alarm* request) arrives.

Other System Calls

```
sync()
```

sync requests that all pending block output be completed, so that file systems are made consistent. It is normally executed automatically every 30 seconds by the *update* process, but should be invoked explicitly (by the *sync* command from the shell) before halting the machine in single-user mode.

```
mount(filesystem, dirname, readonly)
        char     *filesystem;
        char     *dirname;
        int      readonly;  umount(filesystem)
        char     *filesystem;
```

filesystem is the name of a block-structured special file capable of holding a Unix mountable file system. This file system is attached to the existing directory hierarchy so that the directory name *dirname* (which must already exist) now refers to the root directory of the mounted file system. If *readonly* is set, no write operations will be allowed on *filesystem*. *umount* undoes the work of *mount*. The *mount* call is considerably more complicated under Berkeley Unix, in order to take account of networked file stores and (most recently) automounting of file systems. Some versions of AT&T Unix provide a networked file-store facility called *RFS* (or Remote File Store); the most common form of networked file store under Berkeley Unix is *NFS*, derived from the Network File Store protocol designed by Sun Microsystems. (These protocols are described in more detail in Chapter 13.) On versions of Berkeley Unix that support a distributed file store, and under System VR4, the *mount* call has four arguments, the fourth argument usually providing type-specific information to *mount*. It is difficult to predict what flavour of *mount* call the reader is likely to encounter; however, the general principal is always the same, and the call will usually be similar to the one above.

```
acct(filename)
        char     *filename;
```

If process accounting is available on the system, *acct* makes *filename* the accounting file, into which a record is written for each process that terminates. If *filename* is zero, accounting is turned off.

9.4   UNIX-SPECIFIC LIBRARY FUNCTIONS

For details of how to use these functions, see section 3 of the Programmer's Manual.

```
char *ctime(timelocation)
        long      *timelocation;
struct tm *localtime(timelocation)
        long      *timelocation;
struct tm *gmtime(timelocation)
        long      *timelocation;
char *asctime(timebuffer)
        struct    tm *timebuffer;
char *timezone(zone, dst)
        int       zone;
        int       dst;
```

These manipulate date and time information in various ways. The most frequently used are *ctime*, which returns a printable string representation of the date and time given a time in the form provided by the system call *time*, and *localtime*, which fills a structure with the date and time broken down into integer fields, and returns a pointer to it.

```
char *getenv(name)
        char      *name;
```

name is taken as the name of an environment variable, and the corresponding value returned, or *NULL* if the variable is unset.

```
char *getlogin()
```

getlogin attempts to find the username of the user who started the calling process; if it cannot do so, it returns *NULL*.

```
char *getpass(prompt)
        char      *prompt;
```

getpass reads a password from the terminal, after printing the string *prompt* and turning off echoing of input.

```
getpw(uid, buf)
        char      *buf;
```

getpw fills **buf* with the line of the password file for user ID *uid*. This call has been made obsolete by *getpwent*.

```
struct passwd *getpwent()
struct passwd *getpwuid(uid)
        int       uid;
struct passwd *getpwnam(name)
        char      *name;
setpwent()
endpwent()
```

These obtain information from the password file; a similar collection of functions, with *gr* rather than *pw* in their names, accesses the group file. *getpwuid* obtains the data for a given numerical user ID, while *getpwnam* finds the data for a given username.

```
char *mktemp(template)
        char    *template;
```

mktemp takes *template* as a pattern, and generates from it a name which refers to no existing file. The template is a legal pathname ending in *XXXXXX*; the *X*'s are replaced by the process number and a suffix letter. *mktemp* is used by programs which need to create temporary files, and may be running simultaneously in several processes.

```
nlist(filename, nametable)
        char    *filename;
        struct  nlist nametable;
```

nlist obtains data from the symbol table (or *name list*) of an executable file about the identifiers held in *nametable*. It is used in symbolic debugging aids, and in programs which need to find the core addresses of variables in the Unix kernel.

```
perror(message)
        char    *message;
```

perror prints a brief description of the most recent error incurred by a system call, preceded by the string *message*.

```
FILE *popen(command, accessmode)
        char    *command;
        char    *accessmode;
pclose(pipestream)
        FILE    *pipestream;
```

popen runs the specified Unix *command* after opening a pipe to it open for reading or writing according to whether *accessmode* is "r" or "w". *pclose* closes a stream created by *popen*, and waits for the associated command to finish.

```
sleep(nseconds)
        unsigned nseconds;
```

sleep suspends execution for the specified number of seconds.

```
system(command)
        char    *command;
```

command is executed by a shell started as a sub-process. The caller waits until the shell terminates.

```
char *ttyname(filedescriptor)
        int     filedescriptor;
isatty(filedescriptor)
        int     filedescriptor;
ttyslot()
```

ttyname returns the name of the terminal which has been opened as *filedescriptor*, or *NULL* if it is not a terminal.

isatty returns 1 if the *filedescriptor* is a terminal, 0 otherwise. *ttyslot* returns the line number of the entry in the file */etc/ttys* of the controlling terminal of the calling process.

9.5 PROGRAM DEVELOPMENT AIDS

Debuggers

One of the most valuable tools in program development is a good symbolic debugger; sad to say, many Unix systems do not possess one! The debugger which is supplied with most systems is a program called *adb*. To use *adb* it is necessary to understand something of the architecture of the underlying hardware, since *adb* works at the level of machine instructions. It provides the user with the ability to examine and change the values of variables in a program being debugged, to obtain a traceback of the sequence of function calls which led to a particular state (in particular, a core dump), and to run a program under controlled conditions, stopping at specified breakpoints, or stepping through one machine instruction at a time. It is by no means an easy tool to use, especially for the novice user.

A step towards a better debugger is *dbx*, available with most Berkeley Unix systems, which was derived from an earlier symbolic debugger called *sdb*, (also from University of California at Berkeley) which allows the user to debug her C, Fortran 77, or Pascal program in terms of her own source code. Both *dbx* and *sdb* contain a number of bugs, but are nevertheless useful tools. It is to be hoped that *dbx*, or a similar tool, will be available with future releases of AT&T Unix and other implementations such as OSF.

In addition to *dbx*, a debugger called *gdb* has been developed by the Free Software Foundation to accompany the FSF portable *C* compiler; this compiler produces relatively high-quality code for a variety of machines running Unix, and may be available on your system.

Program Profiling

In programs which are to be heavily used, it is useful to obtain some notion of which parts of the code are executed most frequently, and where the program uses most processor time. It is well known that without such information, trying to speed up a program is unlikely to be at all productive. Making a particular function ten times as fast as before will have no perceptible effect on performance if the function only accounted for 5% of the CPU time in the first place.

Unix provides the facility to obtain such execution profiles. To profile a C program, you should recompile it specifying the option *-p* , e.g.

```
$  cc -p -o myprog myprog.c
```

You then run the program in the normal way; when it finishes, it creates a file called *mon.out* in the current directory. This can be analysed by the command *prof*, which prints statistics on the number of calls to each function, and the average amount of time per call; on most systems, the former statistic is *not* reported for functions from the C library. In the following example, we show only the first few lines of the output of *prof*:

```
$  mysort myfile >mysortedfile
$  prof mysort
time   cumsecs  #call   ms/call   name
28.5     0.88      1     883.85    _sort
19.9     1.50    1106      0.56    _rline
12.4     1.88      1     383.56    _merge
 0.0     2.19    9682      0.03    _cmpa
 7.9     2.44     530      0.46    _qsort
 7.0     2.66                      _write
 5.4     2.82                      _read
 ...
```

prof reports the percentage of the total time taken by each routine, a cumulative total of elapsed time, the number of calls, and the average time per call.

make — Building Programs from Several Source Files

It is convenient when writing a large program to divide it into several separate files to reflect the logically distinct aspects of the program. However, it is clearly not desirable to have to recompile all the separate sources every time any of them is changed, nor to keep track of which files have been changed in the course of a particular alteration, especially since changing one file, such as a header, may mean that other dependent files need to be recompiled. Fortunately, there is a program, *make*, which will do just this task.

The user specifies which of her source files depend upon which others, and how to rebuild an out of date file. *make* will then find out which files need to be rebuilt, and invoke the appropriate shell commands. It also has built-in rules of dependency. For cxample if it needs to rebuild a compiled object file (which by Unix convention always ends in *.o*), and there exists a corresponding file with name ending in *.c*, *make* will by default run the C compiler on the *.c* file.

Although *make* was designed for managing program source files, it can also be used successfully for managing text documents composed of separate files; it is useful, for example, when some but not all the files need to be filtered through *tbl* or *neqn*.

A simple example of a *make* script might be

```
CFLAGS = -O
OBJS = image.o main.o func.o

all:    image

image:  ${OBJS}
        cc ${CFLAGS} -o $@ ${OBJS}

${OBJS}: defs.h global.h

clean:
        rm -f ${OBJS} image core a.out
```

This *make* file begins by defining two variables, *CFLAGS* (which is used by *make* when compiling 'C' programs) and *OBJS*, which defines a list of object file names. The first rule in the file, *all*, is a common notation — if *make* is invoked with no arguments, it will attempt to satisfy the first rule in the file. It is useful to make the first rule a "place holder" that lists all the targets that should normally be built.

The second rule tells *make* that the target called *image* depends upon three object files; if any of these object files are out of date (either because the corresponding source file has been modified, or because the include files listed on line 9 have been modified) the source file will be recompiled using *make*'s built-in rules. When *make* has ensured that all the dependencies for *image* are satisfied it then compares the date on the dependency files against the date on the target file, *image*. If *image* is out of date, the rule that appears on line 7 is invoked to recompile the target file. The string "$@" refers to the current target — in this case, *image*; *make* provides a number of names of this form to allow you to design your own general-purpose rules.

The final rule in this example, on line 11, is an example of a rule without any targets; this implies a rule that is never satisfied, so the attached command will always be executed. In this example, *clean* does not appear in the default rule (fortunately!), but it can be invoked by entering *make clean*. Rules like this can be extremely useful for performing "administrative" duties.

Program Maintenance

In a large software development project, it can require substantial effort to keep track of changes made to a system, particularly as several users may simultaneously be working on different parts of it. The *sccs* and *rcs* systems provide a means of managing the multiple versions of software which arise out of such development, making it possible to retain a history of all changes made, recover earlier versions, and keep track of parallel streams of development carried out by different users.

sccs is not available on Unix Version 7, but is available on System III and later releases from AT&T, as well as on several other derived Unix systems. *rcs* was designed by Walter Tichy, and was designed to avoid the problems encountered with *sccs*. It is somewhat easier to use than *sccs*, and has been adopted by (and is distributed by) the Free Software Foundation. Many Unix suppliers (although not all) include a copy of *rcs* in their software distributions.

A Final Note on Type Checking

C is extremely lax about data types; it will permit almost any type to be treated as almost any other, and will rarely even issue warnings, although the version of the language currently being approved by ANSI incorporates much stricter type checking facilities. For those who want to take advantage of the benefits of a strongly typed language, and are obliged to use the old version of *C*, there exists a program, *lint*, which enforces strict type rules and checks that function arguments are used consistently, and that the code is as far as possible self-consistent and portable. *lint* is an excellent tool for identifying potential bugs, although it can be irritating at times, since it is virtually impossible to force it to ignore certain usages which you know perfectly well will behave correctly, even though beyond the letter of *lint*'s law.

Chapter 10

Administration and Maintenance

All computer systems ultimately need managing; in some environments the management will be all pervading while in others it may be so informal as to be invisible to most users. Whichever, responsibility has to be taken somewhere and Unix provides a variety of utilities and special files to support these essential functions. We shall tour here through the indispensable parts of Unix system management; in most of what follows, access to the programs and files described, or at least write access, is limited to the user *root* who wields Super-user privilege. It is clearly not good practice for ordinary users to have permission to change other users' access at will.

10.1 ADDING USERS

Usernames do not appear on the system by magic; each new username, with associated password and directory, has to be explicitly entered by the system administrator. Users are characterised by four essential features; *name, group*, (initial) *password* and *login directory* each of which is entered in the file */etc/passwd*, together with other useful information about the user like telephone and office number. In fact a user is also characterised by an integer unique to her, her *user number* (often called *user ID*); this too appears in */etc/passwd*. The *name* is held literally, the *password* in encrypted form (necessarily so, since */etc/passwd* is generally readable by everybody) and the *group* as a number. The file */etc/group* contains the index of groups and relates them to the numbers used in */etc/passwd* — this file too is maintained by the system management.

Each line in */etc/passwd* represents an entry for one user; within such an entry the individual pieces of data are separated by colons. The order these data are held in is

Username
Encrypted password
User number

Group number
Private information — e.g., name, phone number
Login directory
Default shell

Thus an example entry might be

```
dcs:password:293:20:D.C.Stephens,3.12A,x5744:/usr/staff/dcs:
```

This user would log in with the name *dcs*; we do not know what her password is, only to what the system has encrypted it. *dcs*'s user number, which is unique and referenced by other system accounting programs, is *293* and her group number is *20*. Personal information is often used by "lookup" utilities — in this example the real name, preferred name, office number and phone number are recorded. The login directory for this user is */usr/staff/dcs* (so we may guess that the group of this user is *staff*), and her login shell (since it does not appear explicitly) will be the default shell for the system. Notice that this gives the system manager power to decide which shell a particular user shall run at login; this can be a powerful way of tailoring a user community. The default is */bin/sh.*

The existence of this entry, the login directory and the knowledge of the password are all that the user needs to log in to and use Unix. Power to edit this file is thus all that is required to maintain the user list; customarily all users will have read access to it, but only user *root* will have write access.

Removing a user is a simple matter of deleting the relevant line in */etc/passwd* and removing her directory and its contents; system managers need to be cautious in their approach to deleting users — a reasonable technique is never to re-use user *ID*'s; as new users are added, they are added at the end of the */etc/passwd* file. This avoids any possibility of the files of a new user becoming mixed up with any undeleted files of an old user.

Adding a user is the reverse — a line needs to be edited in or appended to the file, and the default directory needs creating. This is not, of course, straightforward in the case of the password; whatever the user chooses as her initial password (or whatever the system manager decrees it shall be) is not entered explicitly but must be encrypted; do this using the program *passwd*. Without an argument this program amends your own password, but if supplied a username as argument it will, provided the calling user has sufficient privilege, change that user's password. The conversation will look like this;

```
# passwd username
New password:
Retype new password:
```

For the usual security reasons, there will be no echo.

It is customary to collect the user installation procedure into a shell script. This should perform the edit to */etc/passwd*, install a defined password and create the new directory. It is good practice when performing this kind of procedure to take a copy of */etc/passwd* before editing, allowing recreation of the user list before amendment in the event of disaster (for example, a system crash during the edit or a faulty shell script).

Many Unix systems provide an editing utility called *vipw* which performs a number of tests on the format of the password file after it has been edited; at a minimum, it will usually check the format of the *root* entry to ensure that there is at least one valid entry.

10.2   GROUP MEMBERSHIP

Another login characteristic in the gift of the system manager is multiple group membership; new users are assigned to a group via their entry in */etc/passwd*, but if their username also appears after any other group names in the file */etc/group* then they are deemed to be a member of those groups too. Under AT&T Unix, users can change group during a session by means of the command *newgrp*; under Berkeley Unix, a user can be in up to eight groups or sixteen groups simultaneously, depending upon the Unix version.

This feature is a frill of which use is not often made on Unix systems.

10.3   FILE OWNERSHIP

Two more utilities exist governing users and their files whose use is usually restricted to the system manager. Frequently files will be put into directories having the wrong ownership characteristics; this usually happens when they are copied from one directory to another, and often results in users having unreadable files cluttering up their directories, simply because the access parameters are wrong. What is required is that such files' ownership be changed to that of the directory's owner, or at least that the files *group* ownership be changed to that of the directory's owner. The programs *chown* and *chgrp* exist to do this; thus

```
$   chown jim FILE
```

will change the ownership of *FILE* to *jim*, whatever it was before and

```
$   chgrp pg FILE
```

will change the *group* ownership of *FILE* to *pg*; either program will take the numeric identification (as provided by */etc/passwd* or */etc/group*) instead of the literal name. On some versions of Unix, such as System V.3, *chown* can be executed by any user, thus allowing users to donate files to other users; other versions of Unix allow only the super-user to change the ownership of files.

Recent versions of Berkeley Unix provide the extremely useful feature of a recursive option to *chown* and *chgrp*; quite often, they will also allow *chown* to specify both the owner and the group by separating the two with a '.'. For example,

```
$   chown -R diane.staff henry/data
```

will change the owner and group of all the files and directories below *henry/data*.

10.4   FILE SYSTEMS

Many of the file systems that comprise Unix reside permanently — for example, */usr, /bin, /etc* and */tmp* will always be there. User areas, however, will almost certainly contain large sub-structures; these may represent logical partitions of a physical disk, or quite plausibly be physical structures in their own right. The directory structure of Unix permits new structures to be added to any point of the directory tree, and a variety of utilities exist to create, mount, remove and watch over these structures.

Most of what we shall meet in this section is described fully in the Unix manual; administrators intending to manipulate file systems should understand what follows and then work with a copy of the manual to hand. It is also important to bear in mind that these details may vary considerably from one version of Unix to another.

Creating filesystems uses either the program *mkfs* or the program *newfs* — file systems can be created so that they begin life totally empty, or with a *boot block* to enable Unix to be loaded, or with a skeleton file tree. *newfs* makes use of the geometry of the disk (in other words, the layout of the sectors, tracks and surfaces and the speed of rotation) to call *mkfs* with a set of optimal parameters — in effect, it is simply a front-end to *mkfs*; the parameters to *mkfs* vary a great deal from one version of Unix to another, but it needs to know a variety of specialised information, in particular the size of the new system and, if the structure is physical, its geometry. An example might be

```
$  mkfs /dev/xy0g N
```

which would create an empty file system *dev/xy0g* of size *N* blocks, create a table of information containing all the critical information describing the file system (referred to as the *superblock*) initialise the i-node table (which contains all the information relating to the files) and the free-block tables (which allow Unix to locate all of the unoccupied areas within the file system). Depending on the precise way in which it was called, it may also create some files. The name of the file structure is dependent on a variety of factors; its parent physical device, and the section of that device on which it resides in particular. These are considerations only resolved with a full knowledge of the local configuration.

Once a filesystem has been made with *newfs* or *mkfs*, it may be mounted — made available to the system — with *mount*. *mount* needs to know the name of the file structure (defined by *mkfs*) and the destination directory (the point on the directory tree at which the structure is to be mounted).

Before a file system is mounted, however, it should be validated. During day-to-day use of the system a number of inconsistencies can occur — notably these appear after a system crash when Unix's internal housekeeping is unable to perform its proper function. These problems may result in the list of files on a structure not reflecting the actual file store (meaning that the *i-node* list is damaged), or in there being some unusable portion of the structure. The program *fsck* performs a file system check to resolve these inconsistencies.

At this point it is worth noting that any disk partition can be accessed in one of two ways — either as a *block* device, with a name of the form */dev/xy0g*, or as a *raw* device (also known as a *character special* device); the name of the raw device is almost invariably the name of the block device prefixed by an "r" (for example, */dev/rxy0g*). For efficiency reasons *fsck* is usually run on the raw device.

It is also worth noting that when a file system is mounted Unix stores quite a lot of information about the file system in memory, including most of the superblock together with a list of all the i-nodes corresponding to open files. As a result, you must be careful when running *fsck* to run it on an unmounted file system. In order to correct a corrupted file system, *fsck* makes changes directly to the information on disk — if the file system were mounted, Unix might update the superblock and i-node list from the information held in memory, at which point the file system has probably been corrupted again. When a Unix system is bootstrapped, *fsck* is usually run on the root file system very early in the bootstrap process. If any errors are found in the root file system they must be corrected and the machine must be halted and the bootstrap restarted in order for the corrections to be retained.

fsck is usually run automatically by Unix at startup time on all mounted structures, but system administrators may run it interactively at any time; for example

```
$  fsck /dev/rxy0g
```

would check the integrity of structure */dev/xy0g*, although this task would almost always be performed with */dev/xy0g* unmounted for the reasons explained above, or in *single-user* mode (see Section 10.11).

A variety of program options permit automatic patching up of problems that manifest themselves, or consultation of the operator over alterations made to the structure to resolve difficulties.

When *fsck* is not available (usually on systems derived from Version 7), its place is often taken by a collection of more elementary and less powerful programs: *icheck*, *ncheck*, *dcheck*, and *clri*. Their use is described in the Programmer's Manual. In general, it is not possible to recover lost files using these; many systems also possess *ipatch* which allows more detailed adjustment of an i-node.

For example, the commands

```
$  fsck /dev/xy0g
...output from fsck ...
$  mount /dev/xy0g /usr/pg/jim
```

would have the effect of validating and then mounting the file structure
/dev/xy0g, with whatever it contains, at the directory */usr/pg/jim*. More
recent versions of Unix provide a mapping between file systems and positions in the directory tree — a Berkeley Unix system will contain a file
named */etc/fstab* containing something like this:

```
/dev/xy0a / 4.2 rw 1 1
/dev/xy0h /usr 4.2 rw 1 4
/dev/xy0d /usr/users 4.2 rw 1 2
```

which gives the name of the file system, its default position in the directory tree and a list of options. This allows the user to type

```
$  mount /usr/users
```

instead of using the literal name "/dev/xy0d". If your Unix system supports a distributed file-store, *mount* will allow you to attach part of the
file system on another machine to your local file system. For example,
the command

```
$  mount cray2:/usr/users/imagedata /usr/imagedata
```

will mount the directory tree called */usr/users/imagedata* residing on
the remote system called *cray2* onto the local directory */usr/imagedata*.
(This example uses the *Networked File Store* protocol, discussed in section 13.3.)

umount is the inverse of *mount*, so to remove a file system we may
say

```
$  umount /dev/xy0g
```

It is a well-known fact among computer users that the demand for file
storage of users always exceeds the supply available; this usually results
in sophisticated systems of restriction on users preventing them creating
more files than the available space can accommodate. Some versions of
Unix now support *quota management*, where the amount of disk space

that a user can occupy is laid down by the system manager and can usually be set on a per-user basis — if a user approaches the limit of her quota she will receive a warning; if she then proceeds to exceed her quota, the system will usually prevent her from creating any further files or adding to the files that currently exist. Even if a Unix system does not support quota management, there are two standard tools that are provided for checking filestore usage. *du* catalogues disk usage of files and directories from a given point on a directory tree downwards and *quot* counts the number of blocks and files owned on particular structures by particular users. Unfortunately, *du*, while smart enough to count a file only once regardless of the number of links to it, cannot tie files to owners, while *quot* can count the number of files and their size, but not record their names. Individual sites are left to devise the most locally suitable way of combining these two to give the best picture of individual user usage statistics.

10.5 TAPES - ARCHIVING AND RESTORING

Magnetic tape is an indispensable medium for the traffic and long term storage of files. Frequently users will want to move data or programs from one site to another and it avails them nothing that both may run Unix if there is no physical mechanism for moving the files; in general this will mean a tape. Other uses of tapes are legion — highly managed systems will indulge in frequent "dumps" of their filestores in order that everything may be restored in the event of catastrophe. Such dumps may be of the whole system, or of files modified recently (so called incremental dumps). Tapes also provide a solution to the space-shortage problem — very commonly files that have not been accessed for some time will be removed from disk to magnetic tape until the user requires them online again.

Recalling that Unix views tape drives as files, we see that it is possible to conduct all tape usage with commands such as *cat*, so

```
$ cat FILE >/dev/mt0
```

would write *FILE* from the current directory to the tape currently loaded on device */dev/mt0*. This is a perfectly legitimate way of storing data on tape, but it does not permit disciplined dumping and archiving.

The recommended tape archiving utility under System V is *cpio*, while under Berkeley Unix it is *tar*; the *tar* tape archiver is the accepted way of carrying tapes between Unix systems; indeed any *tar* produced tape may be expected to be readable at any Unix site sporting a tape drive that is physically compatible. At its simplest, *tar* requires to know only the names of files you are interested in and whether they are to be written to or read from the tape; thus

```
$ tar c *
```

(invoking the *c* option) writes all files in the current directory, and all subdirectories, to the tape, while

```
$ tar x FILE
```

(invoking the *x* option) will extract *FILE* from the tape into the current directory.

You should try to avoid creating *tar* tapes using absolute path names (i.e, path names that begin with '/'); if a file or directory is stored on a *tar* tape using a relative path name, it can be restored at any position in the directory tree; a file or directory with an absolute path name, however, can only be restored to the same position in the directory tree that it originally came from. This can be a considerable nuisance.

It can be disconcerting watching tapes whirl away silently so *tar* provides a mountain of options to log its progress; prospective archivers should work with a manual close at hand.

tar selects a default density by using a default tape drive — Unix allows the user to select between tape densities by using a variety of device names; some of the more common names are */dev/mt0* (800bpi), */dev/mt8* (1600bpi) and, more recently, */dev/mt12* (6250bpi). For definitive information, the user should consult the manuals for her local version of Unix. *tar* usually selects 1600bpi, and has a concept of a *default tape drive* for sites possessing more than one — these defaults are installation dependent and should be determined in advance if you need to know the tape's write density or to be selective about tape drives.

For backing up entire file systems, the other essential tape utility is *dump*, used for dumping file systems; this utility is available on Version 7 Unix and on Berkeley versions of Unix, but on AT&T System V it has been replaced by *cpio* which, coupled with *find*, allows the user to dump files selectively on to magnetic tape. With *dump* it is customary to have various "levels" of dump reflecting various dates of file creation or modification — thus a dump of files up to a day old may be quite short while a dump of files created over the last ten years will almost certainly be a full system (or *epoch*) dump, and may be expected to take some time. *dump* can dump at ten such levels which are keyed by digits; these will be translated to dates in the file *dumpdates* which is usually kept in the directory */etc*.

Disciplined use of *dump* should insure users against accidental deletion of valued files. When this happens, the system administrator should identify which tape written by *dump* holds the latest version of the file that has been lost, then use the utility *restor* (or *restore*) to fetch it back. *restor* is the Version 7 utility; *restore* is the extended Berkeley version of the same utility. *restor* is written especially to read back dump tapes; it may, on rare occasions, be used to read back a whole dump (this is one way to copy a file system from one physical structure to another) but is more often used to read back files selectively. Unfortunately, *restor* and *restore* work very differently — when doing a complete restore, *restor* works on an **unmounted** file system, since it manipulates the i-node list directly; when restoring individual files, *restor* works on a **mounted** file system, fetching the file from tape and giving it a name corresponding to the i-node number of the file at the time the file was dumped. Unlike *restor*, *restore* always works on a mounted file system, and extracts files using the relative path of the file name instead of the i-node number. It is important to sit down with the manuals for *dump*, *restor*, *restore* and *cpio* before making serious use of them.

10.6 SPOOLERS

Under Version 7 Unix, spooling (of, for example, lineprinters) was quite unstandardised; with the advent of the Berkeley and System V versions, spooling software is usually available. The spooling system under Berkeley Unix is implemented on top of the *socket* mechanism (see Chapter 13); under System V, the spooler is usually based upon either *named pipes* or *streams* (again, see Chapter 13). In spooling, the general strategy is to copy files for printing to a "spool directory" which the spooling software will then, in its own good time, transport to the device requested. It is customary for spooling software to provide a number of options — output should be preceded by a banner page giving the username and file name, and it is common for a simple option to be available to permit printing of multiple copies. A variety of pre-printer filters is also an essential to translate special constructs, for example backspaces and underlining, into a form that the device can understand. It is usually possible for a system manager to interpose local spooling software into the spooling system — for example, a PostScript printer might require a more complex negotiation with the host computer than a simpler high-speed band printer.

10.7   FILES TO MAINTAIN — *motd*, *ttytab* AND *ttys*

Most days the system manager will have some essential information for users; impending downtime, device availability and so on. These are entered in the file */etc/motd* (**message of the day**). Every time users log in this file is printed on the terminal; any editor may be used to put information in */etc/motd* — all that is necessary is to ensure it has read access for all users; write access is generally restricted to administration personnel.

   /etc/ttytab and */etc/ttys* provides a mechanism for controlling terminal access. */etc/ttys* will usually contain a one line entry for each terminal on the system, consisting of its name (as it appears in */dev*) preceded by a two digit code. The first digit may be 0 or 1; 0 will cause the entry to be ignored, thus disabling the terminal. The second digit determines the baud (speed) and other characteristics of the terminal; generally a zero here means a 300 baud dial-up line but anything else is site dependent. The program *init* refers to this file and passes a terminal's entry to a *line listener* (usually the program *getty*) which has the task of listening for login requests on the appropriate line. To see the full range of selectable baud rates on older versions of Unix, refer to the *getty* source code; on more recent versions of Unix the speed and login "banner" are defined in a system file that is read by *getty*, thus allowing the super-user to add new terminal speeds and login banners to a system without modifying *getty*. On Berkeley Unix, this file is called *gettytab* and usually lives in the */etc* directory. Should the *ttys* file ever be modified, it will be necessary to ensure that *init* has seen the alteration before it will be implemented on the terminal; on *some* versions of Unix this may be accomplished by sending it the *hangup* signal (signal *1*) with the *kill* command thus

```
$  kill -1 1
```

(*init* will always have process number 1). Be sure of what you are doing before issuing this command; on some versions (in particular pure Version 7 Unix) this will switch the system to single-user mode.

Some versions of Unix use the */etc/ttytab* file instead of the */etc/ttys* file — the format is more complex than the format of */etc/ttys*, and it provides the system administrator with a finer degree of control. A line in the */etc/ttytab* file consists of a device name (as it appears in */dev*), the command to invoke to listen for login attempts (usually */etc/getty*), a description of the terminal type and the word *on* or the word *off* (to indicate whether the line is active or not). Some versions of Unix allow additional information at the end of the line; often, the presence or absence of the word *secure* indicates whether is is safe for root to login on that line.

Some versions of Unix implement *init* as a *state machine* — *init* can be in one of a number of distinct *states* or *modes*, each mode being appropriate to a particular state of the system. For example, there could be a state for startup (or restart), a state for shutdown, and a state for normal multi-user operation. In this case, the file *inittab* will contain a description of each of the states, together with a list of the terminals that will be active while the system is in each of the states.

10.8 PROGRAMS THAT CONTROL SYSTEM ACCESS

Users cannot log in and out of Unix without the supporting programs *init*, *getty* and *login*. *init* and *getty* will live in */etc* — *login* will usually live in */bin*. Of these, the most essential is *init* which is invoked as the last stage of the system startup (bootstrap) procedure; *init*'s duty is to visit each terminal on the system and check its availability. This may mean, for example, ensuring the connection of dial up terminals. Having opened the terminal for read and write access, *init* runs *getty*, giving it as argument the second digit of the terminal's entry in */etc/ttys* — it is thus that the terminal's baud rate is established. *getty* will now sit idle on the terminal awaiting a user; when you approach a free terminal it is *getty* producing the message

```
login:
```

When a user types a name, valid or not, *getty* reads the name and passes it to *login* — a distinct and separate program. *login*'s action is to take the proffered name and request a password — this will then be checked against the (encrypted) form found in */etc/passwd* and, if there is a match, *login* starts up a shell and lets the user in. If the password is incorrect, or the username invalid, the message

```
Login incorrect
```

will appear, and the username re-prompted for. Notice that this time the

```
login:
```

prompt is coming from *login*, not *getty*.

After a successful login, *login* will make an entry in the files */etc/utmp* and */usr/adm/wtmp*; the former keeps a record of all users currently logged in, the latter a complete login history. These files are accessed by useful programs like *who* and other system accounting utilities.

When a login shell exits, control of the terminal is returned to the *init* process, which tidily removes the user's entry in the */etc/utmp* log file, records in */usr/adm/wtmp* that a logout has occurred on that terminal and hands the terminal back to *getty* to make it available to the next user.

It can be seen that no part of the login/logout procedure may operate without all three of these programs being present; the system can (just) function without *getty* and *login* but *init* is an essential. Should *init* die at any time, the system will probably crash, and at the least behave very oddly. So seriously is the death of *init* regarded that Berkeley Unix will display a panic message and then either halt, or attempt to reboot. On other systems, the observable symptom of *init* dying is that new users will be unable to log in, while those already logged in should be all right for a while.

One other program is useful for maintaining the day-to-day health of the system; *cron*, which runs all the time the system is active, wakes up once per minute and executes any task required of it. These tasks are catalogued in a file */usr/lib/crontab* which is a list of actions, associated with times at which to execute them. Such times are specified as minute, hour, day (of the month), month and/or day (of the week); for example, to maintain a weekday hourly record of who is logged in we may enter in */usr/lib/crontab*

```
0 * * * 1-5 who >> /usr/adm/who.log
```

The asterisks match any time; thus *who* is run on the hour every hour on days one to five (interpreted by *cron* as Monday to Friday), appending its output to */usr/adm/who.log*. There is large scope for the specification of these times — the manual entry should allow you to tailor your local environment to best advantage.

Recent versions of Unix permit individual users to submit requests to *cron*, usually *via* the command *crontab*. The format for *cron* requests (for any user) is usually documented in section 5 of the Unix Programmer's Manual under *crontab*.

10.9 ACCOUNTING

Two programs exist to provide user accounting. The first, *ac*, uses the file */usr/adm/wtmp* that we have already met to compile a record of connect time; options permit this to be broken down on a per day or per user basis.

The other program, *sa* is more elaborate and accesses the log file */usr/adm/acct*, in which an entry is made each time a process terminates, assuming that your version of Unix supports this form of accounting and has initiated it. These entries comprehensively log a user's activity: the command that initiated the process, connect time, processor time, User ID, group ID, terminal and I/O activity. Not surprisingly, the *acct* file is inclined to grow very large; *sa* provides a compressing, summarising facility which deposits the *acct* information in two compacted files, */usr/adm/savacct* and */usr/adm/usracct*. It is normal to perform this compression regularly, for example with *cron*.

sa is a complicated program offering a multitude of options. Administrators should consult the manual to determine how best to run it to account their system most satisfactorily.

10.10 UPDATING SYSTEM PROGRAMS

Some Unix installations are supplied with the source code of the system; with the advent of suppliers offering maintenance of the software this is becoming less widespread, but many manufacturers still offer an option of purchasing a source code licence (usually at a relatively high price). The availability of this source is often excuse enough for programmers to want to amend or tailor the system, although frequently this is a desirable and sensible thing to do when your particular application does not quite fit the design of some program.

You may expect the sources to be found in the directory */usr/src*; the directory structure of */usr/src* will vary considerably from one Unix version to another. Normally, the source code for commands (such as those found in */bin* and */usr/bin*) will be kept in a separate directory from the code libraries (such as those in */lib* and */usr/lib*).

Sites also generate their own system programs to fulfil local requirements; it is good practice to maintain the source of these along with the distributed source — that is, keep them in */usr/src* alongside the others. Local commands and libraries are normally installed in directories such as */usr/local/bin* and */usr/local/lib*.

10.11   SYSTEM STARTUP AND SHUTDOWN

It is impossible to say much specific about starting up — bootstrapping — and shutting down Unix beyond that both are possible. They are likely to be extremely site dependent, referring to local configuration and local practice.

Startup, once initiated, is a semi-automatic process governed by scripts with names of the form */etc/rc**. These scripts will do housekeeping tasks that usually consist of checking the filestore integrity (via *fsck* or *icheck* and relations), starting up any spoolers that may be required, mounting file systems clearing out */tmp* and running any network daemons. This running of *fsck* may be expected to be performed in *single-user* mode. It is possible to sacrifice all the multi-user features of Unix and devote the system to one user, usually on the system console; this is a highly specialised form of running the system that does not require *getty* or *login* to be active (but does need *init*) since it gives user *root* a shell automatically on the system console and does not use the normal, interactive terminals. Single user operation is usually reserved for patching matters up after catastrophe, for example a conversational running of *fsck* when the file store is in a mess.

Shutdown is accomplished via the *shutdown* command, whose action may well be site dependent, but whose important features are to provide users with periodic warnings up to the specified shutdown time, when interactive use of the system is halted and *init* brings Unix to single-user mode. This is the clean way of bringing the system to the management's mercy — having reached single user state in this polite fashion, administrators should issue the command *sync* to ensure that anything contained in physical memory is written to disc (*sync* is a very simple program that just implements the *sync* system call — see Chapter 9). After this, they are at liberty to do anything up to and including switching the machine off without damaging user activity or files.

Chapter 11

Text Processing

Unix possesses a powerful collection of tools for the preparation of text documents. The essential tool in any text processing system is, of course, an editor for the entry and subsequent amendment of documents. There are many editors available on different Unix systems; the most common editor is *ex*, introduced in Chapter 3, although there are several other context and screen editors, most notably *emacs*.

However, an editor is only the first part of a text processing suite. Unix also provides a text formatting program, *troff*, similar in general principles to the formatters available on many other systems, such as DEC's RUNOFF. *troff* takes care of such actions as automatically filling lines with text, and inserting spaces to align the right margin, handling multiple typefaces and sizes, and a great many other features. For those users not fortunate enough to have access to a phototypesetter, laser printer or similar device, there is a modified version of *troff* called *nroff*, which produces output for devices such as terminals, lineprinters, and daisy-wheel printers. There is also a version of *troff*, called *ditroff*, which produces device-independent output. The output file can be converted for printing on a wide variety of devices, from high quality dot matrix printers to phototypesetters.

Although *troff* is a powerful tool indeed, it is by no means easy to make use of its more advanced features, owing to their complexity. To make it easier to produce documents, *troff* is accompanied by a selection of *macro packages*, that is, collections of *troff* instructions which augment the repertoire of basic commands with more powerful, higher-level commands for paragraphing, automatic section-numbering, footnotes, and other facilities. There are several macro packages available; probably the most widely known are the *ms* macros, which are standard on System V and Berkeley Unix, and are used for most of the Unix documentation, the *man* macros, used for laying out the entries in the Unix manual, the *mm* macros, which are standard in Systems III and V, (and are slowly superseding the *ms* macros) and the *me* macros, from the University of California at Berkeley. We shall describe some of the features of the *ms* macros here, since they are probably the most widely used at the time of writing; once one macro package has been mastered, it is easy to pick up others.

We shall not try to give an exhaustive account of *troff* and the *ms* macros; they are well described in two tutorials in the Unix manuals [8]: *A TROFF Tutorial* [7] and *Using the –ms macros with Nroff and Troff* [12]. Instead, we shall give an introduction to straightforward use of *nroff*; once you have started to use the system, your own needs should lead you to find out which of the more advanced features are relevant to you, and to go to the manual for an account of them.

After describing *nroff*, we shall take a brief look at some related tools, which help in formatting complex tables, mathematical text, and bibliographic references, and also at spelling and style checking programs.

Although the following section describes the use of *nroff*, almost all of the comments are equally applicable to *troff*. Where explicit differences occur, they are noted.

11.1   USING *nroff*

An input file for *nroff* or *troff* consists of the text to be formatted, interspersed with instructions on how to lay it out. The layout of the text in the input file is largely irrelevant to the result; it is the interspersed layout instructions which matter. These instructions usually consist of 2-letter commands appearing at the *start* of a line, preceded by a dot. For example, the command *.bp* instructs *nroff* to begin a new page. Unless you explicitly ask for text to be copied literally from input to output, *nroff* will always fill lines with as many words as will fit, and adjust the spacing so that the right margin is aligned. Thus for example, suppose the file *myfile.n* contains the text

```
This is a short piece of text designed to show
what happens if
you run nroff on text with no interspersed
commands.
Note that the right margin is neatly aligned.
Of course, normally you will want to insert
left and right margins,
paragraphing, sections, page numbers and so on.
```

Then the command

```
$ nroff myfile.n
```

will produce on your terminal the output

> This is a short piece of text designed to show what hap-
> pens if you run nroff on text with no interspersed commands.
> Note that the right margin is neatly aligned. Of course, nor-
> mally you will want to insert left and right margins, para-
> graphing, sections, page numbers and so on.

followed by a lot of blank lines; *nroff* fills the final page with enough blank space to reach the bottom of a page, normally assumed to be 66 lines long.[1]

For historical reasons, if you invoke *troff* with no arguments other than the file name it will attempt to send the results to a CAT/4 typesetter on */dev/cat*. Since very few people possess a CAT/4 typesetter, this is not particularly useful. However, you can ask *troff* to redirect the output to a file for further processing or translation.

The most useful of the many *nroff* commands are

.br *Break*: force a new-line at this point in the text;

.sp *Space*: insert some blank space; e.g. the command **.sp 2** will ask for 2 blank lines to be inserted;

.ls *Line Spacing*: e.g. **.ls 2** asks for all subsequent text to be double-spaced;

.na *No Adjust*: turn off the adjusting of text to align the right margin;

.bp *Begin Page.*

Most of the other *nroff* commands should not be used directly when you are making use of packages such as *ms*, which take over most of the responsibility for low-level tasks such as page-numbering and margin-setting from you. Of course, you do not have to use a macro package; you may wish to define your own high-level formatting commands, or do without altogether, in which case you will need to consult the detailed documentation in the *nroff/troff* manual [14]. However, although it is sometimes annoyingly difficult to persuade the macro package of your choice to lay out text *exactly* the way that you want it, there is no doubt that using a package usually saves a great deal of trouble.

---

[1]This is the standard length for a lineprinter page.

11.2   THE *ms* PACKAGE

To load the *ms* macros, use the option "*-ms*" when you run *nroff*, e.g.

```
$  nroff -ms mytext.n
```

Similarly, you can use "*-mm*", "*-man*", or "*-me*" to load the corresponding package.

The *ms* package was designed for producing manuscripts such as technical reports at Bell Telephone Laboratories. It displays some of its ancestry in the provision of various macros which set out a title page in Bell Laboratories Memorandum format, or which provide the names of various Bell Laboratories sites. Despite this parochialism, most of the package is entirely general-purpose, and can be used for producing more or less any sort of document.

The *ms* commands appear exactly like *nroff* commands, except that they use capital letters for their names, whereas *nroff* uses lower-case names. Some of the more useful commands are:

.PP *Paragraph*; a new paragraph, with indented first line, is started, after leaving a blank line;

.LP *Left Paragraph*; like **.PP**, but not indented;

.IP *Indented Paragraph*; this is like **.LP**, except that the left margin is moved in, and a *tag* can be appended to the paragraph. It is useful for producing lists (like the present one)—this paragraph could be produced by the text:

```
.IP \fB.IP\fR
\fIIndented Paragraph\fR;
this is like \fB.LP\fR,
except that the left margin is moved in,
and a \fItag\fR can be appended to the paragraph.
It is useful for producing lists
(like the present one)
- this
paragraph could be produced by the text:
```

(the interspersed \fR, \fB, and \fI symbols switch to Roman type, boldface, and italics respectively, if you are using *troff*; if you are using *nroff* the results will depend upon the printing device).

.DS *Display*; all text up to the command **.DE** is copied literally, without margin adjustment or filling of lines. The display can be indented from the current left margin (the default), aligned with the left margin (**.DS L**), centred as a block between the margins (**.DS B**), or printed with each individual line centred (**.DS C**).

.KS *Keep Space*; all text up to the command **.KE** is treated as a unit; if the whole text will not fit on the current page, then a new page is started.

.ND *No Date*; suppress the printing of the current date, which the *ms* package normally inserts at the bottom of each page.

.FS *Start Footnote*; text up to the command **.FE** is inserted as a footnote at the bottom of the current page. If it will not fit there, then it is continued at the bottom of the following page. In *troff*, footnotes are normally printed in smaller type than the main text.

.I *Italic font*: appearing on its own, **.I** changes the current font to italic (underlined in *nroff*). If it is used with an argument, then just that argument is italicised, e.g. **.I emphasis** will print as *emphasis*.

.B *Bold font*: similar to **.I** (no effect in *nroff*).

.R *Roman font*: similar to **.I**. Roman is the normal "plain" font used in most documents.

.SH *Section Heading*; text up to the next paragraph beginning is taken as a heading, to be displayed in boldface with surrounding blank lines.

There are many other commands available, described in the *ms* tutorial; however, those given above should suffice for formatting many simple documents.

In addition to the commands, *ms* defines several *number registers* and *string registers* which contain values such as the text of the page headers, the current settings of page margins, and the amount of indentation and separation required to mark the start of a paragraph. These can be altered using the *nroff* commands **.nr** (alter the value in a number register) and **.ds** (define a string).

11.3 PREPROCESSORS FOR *nroff*

Powerful as it is, *nroff* is not well-suited to such tasks as the layout of complex mathematical text or tables. These can be done by using suitable *preprocessors* which read an input file containing high-level descriptions of equations, tables, etc., and generate from them the appropriate *nroff* commands to display them properly. If you do not specify a filename for *nroff* to process, it will read from its standard input (i.e. it can be used as a *filter*). Hence, it is possible to construct a pipeline to pass the output from one or more preprocessors to *nroff*.

There are three particularly useful preprocessors available on most Unix systems: *tbl* which lays out tables, *neqn* which formats mathematical text, and *refer* which processes bibliographic references. We will look briefly at each of these.

11.4 THE *tbl* PREPROCESSOR FOR TABLES

tbl is a program which transforms a description of a table layout, such as

```
.TS
center box tab(%);
lb | cb
l | li.
Program%Function
_
nroff%Text layout
tbl%Format tables
neqn%Format mathematical text
refer%Process bibliography
.TE
```

into the *nroff* commands to produce the table as

Program	Function
nroff	*Text layout*
tbl	*Format tables*
neqn	*Format mathematical text*
refer	*Process bibliography*

Table descriptions are surrounded by the commands **.TS** and **.TE**. Between these comes the description of the layout and contents of the table, which is divided into three parts: options, format and data.

The *options* are used to describe whether the table should be centred on the page, drawn inside a box, expanded to fill the entire page width, and so on. In the above example we have specified that the table be centred (**center**, only the U.S. spelling accepted!), and enclosed in a box (**box**), and that the separation character between data columns is a "%" (**tab(%)**) (the default separation character is a TAB (^I)). The options are ended by a semicolon.

The *format* description follows the options. It consists of a series of lines, corresponding to the lines of data, with an description of how the columns are to be formatted. As in our example, if there are fewer format lines than data lines, the last format line is repeated as often as necessary. Columns can be *left-adjusted* (format **l**), *right-adjusted* (**r**), *centred* (**c**), or *numeric* (**n**), i.e. aligned on the position of a decimal point. Any of these can be followed by a **b** or **i** to indicate that the data in this column should be in boldface or italics, or by a **w(n)** to force the column width to be *n* units. A vertical bar asks for a vertical line to be drawn between columns.

The *data* then follow; the columns of the table are separated by the character specified by the **tab** option, and each line of data corresponds to a line of the table, in general. A line consisting of a single underscore, "_", or equals, "=", can be included to request a single or double horizontal line across the table.

Occasionally, you will want *nroff* or *neqn* to process the text for a column; normally it is left exactly as it appears in the data. To achieve this, a data entry can be started with the characters **T{**, and then continued over as many lines as you like, finishing with a line beginning with **T}**. For example the description

```
.TS
center doublebox tab(%);
lb lbw(40)
l l.
Language%Description
=
C%T{
The most widely used language
on Unix systems throughout the
world; Unix itself is
largely written in C.
T}
_
Pascal%T{
A block-structured language descended
from Algol; not particularly well-suited
for systems programming, or for
string manipulation.
T}
_
Spitbol%T{
A dialect of SNOBOL4;
excellent for text handling, but
not widely available on Unix.
T}
.TE
```

will result in a table similar to

Language	Description
C	The most widely used language on Unix systems throughout the world; Unix itself is largely written in C.
Pascal	A block-structured language descended from Algol; not particularly well-suited for systems programming, or for string manipulation.
Spitbol	A dialect of SNOBOL4; excellent for text handling, but not widely available on Unix.

tbl also offers the possibility of spanning some table entries across two or more columns, or vertically over several data lines. For information on these more complex features, you should look at the *tbl* manual [11].

11.5   THE *neqn* PREPROCESSOR FOR MATHEMATICAL TEXT

There are in fact two programs for laying out mathematical text: *eqn* and *neqn*. The former is intended for use with *troff* on a phototypesetter, while the latter is for use with *nroff*. They process identical input formats; however, *neqn* is necessarily less clever than *eqn*, being unable to cope with changes of font or of character size. You should bear in mind that the examples that follow have been typeset; the results would be very similar if you tried them using *troff* or *ditroff*, but the results with *nroff* may be disappointing. As we remarked at the beginning, it depends upon the printer that you are using.

Input for *neqn* is delimited by the commands **.EQ** and **.EN**; between these there appears a description of the text to be printed in a form which corresponds closely to the way that it would be read aloud. Thus, for example, the text

$$x^2 = y^2 + z^2$$

would be produced by the command

```
.EQ
x sup 2 = y sup 2 + z sup 2
.EN
```

and the text

$$\int_{-\infty}^{0} (u + iv)dz = \frac{-iS}{2k^2} = \frac{i\mu S}{2\rho\Omega_3} \tag{11.1}$$

is produced by

```
.EQ I (11.1)
integral from { - infinity } to 0 ~ (u+iv) dz ~=~
- iS over { 2 k sup 2 } ~=~
{ i mu S } over { 2 rho OMEGA sub 3 }
.EN
```

As the second example shows, Greek letters can be incorporated simply by writing their names; the upper case Greek letters are obtained by writing the name in upper case. Of course, in order to gain the benefit of the program, you must have a device capable of printing the various fancy characters; many daisy-wheel printers are capable of at least making a good approximation to them.

If you are using *nroff* and *neqn,* you will need to tell *nroff* what sort of output device to expect, so that it can look up how to print special characters for that device. You can do this with the option **-T**, e.g.

```
$  neqn mathsfile | nroff -ms -Tdiablo > /dev/diablo
```

assuming that you have available, as the device */dev/diablo,* a Diablo printer. Which devices are available, and what they will be called, varies from one installation to another; you should consult your nearest local expert for advice on this.

neqn input is free-format, in that spaces and newlines are ignored; if you want to include spaces in your equation, you need to use the character "~" as a space-marker, as in the example above. Braces ("{"..."}") can be used for grouping items together; thus

```
.EQ
{ 3 cos (b) } over 2
.EN
```

produces

$$\frac{3\cos(b)}{2}$$

whereas

```
.EQ
3 cos (b) over 2
.EN
```

produces

$$3\cos\frac{(b)}{2}$$

The use of *neqn* is well described in the Unix manual [7] with its accompanying tutorial; it is a powerful system, and we have only looked at the bare beginnings in this section.

11.6   VIEWING *neqn* AND *tbl* OUTPUT ON A DUMB TERMINAL

It is useful to be able to look at a draft of your document on a "dumb" VDU; this is quicker, quieter and uses less paper than printing every draft on a hard-copy printer. Unfortunately, most VDUs are not intelligent enough to handle the half-line motions, reverse motions, and fancy characters produced by these programs. *nroff* will usually try to substitute more or less appropriate characters for those which the terminal cannot print, but that still leaves the problem of half-line and reverse motions.

To handle these, a *postprocessor* for *nroff* is available, called *col*. *col* takes as input a file containing reverse motions, etc., and produces an image of it on a dumb terminal or printer; it can be used as a filter in a pipeline after *nroff*, for example

```
$   tbl prettyfile | neqn | nroff -ms | col
```

which will display as close an approximation as possible of the formatted text on the terminal. On some systems there is also a program *colcrt*, from the University of California at Berkeley, which does a better job than *col* of displaying output with superscripts and subscripts.

11.7 BIBLIOGRAPHIC REFERENCES

Many authors of technical papers maintain a computer database of the literature in their field. There exist utilities on Unix to help maintain such a database, to retrieve entries from it, and to incorporate suitably formatted references in *nroff* documents. They are described in the Unix Programmer's manual [11] and [13].

A publication list is an ordinary text file, containing entries such as

```
%T Unix for Users, 2nd Ed.
%A Chris Miller
%A Roger Boyle
%A Andrew Stewart
%D 1990
%I Blackwell Scientific Publications
%C Oxford
```

where the flags **%T**, **%A**, etc., describe various features of the publication; in the example above we have specified Title, Author (three of them), Date of publication, Issuers, and City of publication. Other possible fields include **B**ook or **J**ournal in which the publication appears, **E**ditor, **P**ages cited, and **V**olume number.

To cite a publication from such a list in an *nroff* file another pre-processor, *refer*, is used. Citations are bracketed by the commands .[and .]; in between come a selection of keywords sufficient to identify the publication uniquely. Thus the above example could be cited as

```
.[
boyle miller stewart unix for users
.]
```

or

```
.[
unix blackwell oxford 1990
.]
```

refer has options allowing you to include references as footnotes, or to save them up until the end of a document and then print them sorted by author-name or by some other key, and giving several choices for the format of the reference itself, such as a label made up from the author and date, or a number, as used in many publications.

It is by no means uncommon to use all the preprocessors described above in a single document; indeed, this chapter is itself such a document! The command needed to process and print it is either

```
$   refer  s -b -p refs ch11 | tbl | neqn | \
            nroff -ms | col | lpr
```

for lineprinter output, using the print-spooling command *lpr* , or

```
$   refer -s -b -p refs ch11 | tbl | eqn | troff -ms
```

if a phototypesetter is available. The options used here for *refer* are:

-s : save references until the end, and then print them sorted by author-name;

-b : leave the text bare at the point where the citation is made; alternatives are available to build a citation automatically from the author's name and the publication date, or to number references sequentially;

-p refs : use the file *refs* as the publication list.

11.8   CHECKING SPELLING AND USAGE

No matter how powerful the available tools for formatting text, a document will be ruined if the spelling or style is bad. Fortunately, most Unix systems provide a spelling checker, *spell*, and some also provide a rather severe style criticiser, *diction*.

spell takes as input a file of English text, and checks each word in it against a large dictionary. Its output is simply an alphabetical list of words not contained in the dictionary, nor obvious derivatives (such as plural forms) of dictionary words. This has two weaknesses, of course. First, *spell* is only as good as its dictionary; most dictionaries supplied with Unix systems are (hardly surprisingly) strong on technical terminology, but weaker in poetic language. Second, if a mis-spelling happens to result in another legal word, *spell* will not report anything amiss; for example, it will not detect "Unix" being mis-typed as "Unit". Nevertheless, *spell* is an invaluable tool for the first shot at proofreading a draft document, picking up a high proportion of the typographic errors. An annoying "feature" is that you are offered a choice of British or American spellings, but not both at once; this causes problems in a British document quoting from American sources, or vice versa.

diction uses a database of common examples of poor use of English to run through a text file flagging possible instances of bad style, which it prints out in context. It is occasionally extremely stupid in its criticism (for example, it criticises "not universally" as a double negative because of the "not un..."'), and you are, of course, entirely free to disagree with the judgement of the author of *diction*'s database, but it is effective at picking up at least some of the weaknesses in usage. If you do not understand why some phrase has been criticised, there is another program, *explain*, which interactively prompts you for a phrase, and then tells you what to use instead.

Consider for example the following paragraph, assumed to be in *my-file*:

> This paragrap contains a few typographical errors and rather a lot of clumsy or unstilish phrases. Although diction is not perfecl, nor absolutely complete, it is, basically, adequate enough to comment on text in the absence of a better alternative.

Running *spell* results in the following dialogue

```
$ spell -b myfile
paragrap
perfecl
unstilish
$
```

while *diction* and *explain* respond as follows:

```
$ diction myfile
myfile
this paragrap contains
a few typographical errors
and[ rather ]a lot of clumsy
or unstilish phrases.

although diction is not perfecl
nor[ absolutely complete ]
it is [ basically ][ adequate
enough ]to comment on text in the
absence of a better alternative.

number of sentences 2 number of hits 4
$ explain
phrase?
rather
use "interesting" for "rather interesting"
use "" for "rather"
phrase?
absolutely complete
use " complete" for "absolutely complete"
phrase?
basically
use "" for "basically"
phrase?
adequate enough
use "adequate" for "adequate enough"
phrase?
```

11.9 SUMMARY

This chapter has provided only the sketchiest of introductions to the Unix text processing tools; an entire book could be written on the subject.

As with many complex topics, however, the best way to learn is to do. By using *nroff* and its various satellites you will become familiar with the simple facilities described here, and eventually your requirements for more elaborate layout will lead you to explore the more remote regions described in the Programmer's Manuals for these programs.

Chapter 12

Some Other Software

In this chapter we explore some of the software available on Unix. The list of topics is far from comprehensive, and we have omitted far more than we have had room to include. In particular, there is now a great variety of commercial packages for tasks such as stock control, spreadsheet accounting, financial modelling, database management and so on. There also exist several packages which provide a *menu-driven* interface to Unix commands, providing a simpler interface than the shell.

We shall consider three main topics here: editors, languages and supporting tools. We shall also describe briefly a relational database system, *ingres*, which is probably in wider use on Unix than any other.

12.1 EDITORS

In chapter 3 we described *vi* and *ex*, and remarked that *ed* is the lowest common denominator of Unix editors. We shall now swing to the other end of the spectrum and look at some alternative editors. It is true to say that editors breed (more precisely, programmers breed editors); whatever facilities a particular flavour of *ed*, *ex*, *vi* or any other editor provides, someone is not going to like it. The editors will then be amended or maybe entirely rewritten; this has resulted in an enormous range being available and one book has not the space (nor three authors the knowledge) to catalogue them all. We summarise here, though, the most popular that are likely to be available.

em

em was developed at Queen Mary College, London, and is a recognition of the fact that *ed*, while suitably simple for beginners, is discouraging in its terseness. Standing for "Editor for Mortals", *em* provides *ed* with prompts, together with one or two extensions. The most useful of these is an intra-line mode. It is certainly to be preferred to *ed*.

185

Queen Mary College have also developed *ded*, which is quite highly regarded although not so widely available. It is a screen editor marketed commercially in the UK.

emacs

emacs is a very advanced screen editor, due to Richard Stallman and James Gosling; it is considerably more powerful than *vi*, offering a split screen facility to permit editing of more than one file simultaneously. You may find it available on systems other then Unix. One of the most popular aspects of *emacs* is that it is possible to extend and modify the commands available to the user *via* a programming language - usually a subset of *LISP*. This makes it possible to customise *emacs* to a wide variety of tasks, from editing of plaintext to reading electronic mail.

There are a number of versions of *emacs* available; the most popular versions are probably Unipress Emacs (based on the version by James Gosling), and GNU Emacs (written by Richard Stallman at the Free Software Foundation).

ned

ned is a screen editor that was originally developed by the RAND Corporation, inside which its evolution has followed a different course to other versions that exist around the world.

ned is quite powerful but does not rival *vi*; experience has shown, however, that it is rather more friendly to the beginner. Like *emacs*, it offers a split screen mode.

sed

sed is a most useful tool; unlike the other editors mentioned here it is not designed to be "interactive", but is a *stream* editor; that is, it will take its commands from a prepared file.

It will be used for files that are too large for comfortable interactive edits, or for edits requiring very complicated commands better prepared in advance, or as an efficient way of performing global functions on a file in a single pass. It is also frequently used as filter in the middle of a pipeline to massage the output of one program into a form suitable for input to another. For example, *sed* could be used to filter out all of the comment lines from a large document, assuming that a comment line is marked by a "#" in column 1:

```
$  sed '/^#/d' < file1 > file2
```

This *sed* command will match any line of text that begins with a "#" and delete it.

12.2 LANGUAGES

The number of languages available on Unix grows almost daily, although only a few are usually distributed as standard. The most common language is, of course, C; some of the Unix-like rewrites which have been implemented in assembler do not offer it, but they are rare. If you hope to exchange software with other Unix sites, C is by far the most portable language available, especially if you avoid using system calls directly as far as possible, and confine yourself to the standard library functions described in Section 3 of the Programmer's Manual.

Assembler

Most systems supply you with an assembler for the underlying processor. However, programming in assembler is rare on Unix, and most assemblers are unsophisticated. Few have any macro-processing capability, and some (e.g. the VAX assembler on Berkeley 4.1bsd) are unfriendly in the extreme. Normally, the assembler is used only to process the code generated by high-level language compilers, for one or two critical library functions and for those few parts of the kernel for which C is inadequate.

Many cross-assemblers are available, for example from Whitesmiths, allowing software for a wide variety of microprocessors to be developed on Unix.

Fortran

Fortran 77 is a standard part of System III and System V from Bell, although it is too large to run on "small" PDP11s (11/30, 11/40, 11/60, etc.). Berkeley Unix is usually supplied with a Fortran compiler called *f77* which conforms closely with the ANSI Fortran standard. Many other systems offer alternative compilers for Fortran, often at extra cost. Some compilers are designed to be compatible with C, so that programs in one can call functions written in the other. The Bell Laboratories and Berkeley *f77*s fall into this class.

There are also available at least two preprocessors, which generate Fortran from a language with C-like control structures: *ratfor* (for **R**ational **F**ortran **D**ialect) and *efl*.

Pascal

There are several implementations of Pascal available, though none is distributed as standard. The most widespread are the system from Berkeley and the one from the Vrije Universiteit, Amsterdam. Each of these supplies both a compiler for efficient execution and an interpreter for quick program testing and extensive diagnostics, together with tools for program tracing and profiling. Also available is *UCSD Pascal*, familiar to many as a single-user operating system on small personal computers.

Other Languages

We simply enumerate the other languages which we know to be available on some Unix systems. There will undoubtedly be omissions from the list.

Ada

The last word (probably) in block-structured languages. Several implementations are in preparation and may be available when you read this chapter; the compiler from the University of York, England, handles a large proportion of the language and generates efficient code for the VAX and Motorola 68000 families of processor.

APL

Available for many versions of Unix.

Awk

A pattern-processing language bearing distant kinship to Snobol, but designed to be particularly useful as a filter in the middle of a pipeline to perform complicated data transformations. The name derives from the initials of the authors (Aho, Weinberger, and Kernighan). There are currently two versions of *awk* available—"old" awk, which is available with System III, System V and most Berkeley distributions, and new awk which supports a number of new features including functions. If, for example, we wished to extract all of the user *ID*s from the password file and sort them into numerical order, we could enter:

```
$   awk 'BEGIN { FS=":" } \
    { print $1 $3 }' < /etc/passwd | sort +1n
```

This pipeline will:

1. read the password file into *awk*, with the Field Separator character set to ":", and print fields 1 and 3. (That is, the user *name* and the user *ID*.)

2. filter the resulting list of names and IDs through *sort*, which will sort the input in numeric order on the second column.

Basic

A rather basic BASIC is available on many Version 7 systems under the name *bas*. More comprehensive systems, usually based on or compatible with DEC BASIC-PLUS systems, are now available for a wide range of machines, although the trend is for BASIC programs to be translated into other, more amenable, languages, usually with the aid of some automatic translation tool.

BCPL

The ancestor of C, and widely used for low-level programming on other systems. It is documented in [15].

Cobol

A variety of commercial Cobol systems are obtainable, though not widely used on Unix systems yet.

Icon

A string processing language in the tradition of Snobol, but more readable. A portable compiler is available for a variety of machines, including the VAX and Motorola 68000 processor families. The language is described in the book by Griswold and Griswold, [6].

Lisp

A list processing language, popular in artificial intelligence. There are several implementations, notably the *Franz Lisp* (interpreter and compiler) from Berkeley, *Kyoto Common Lisp* from the University of Kyoto in Japan and the *Scheme* interpreter from MIT.

Modula-2

The successor to *Pascal*, *Modula-2* offers the structure of Pascal with facilities for dividing up large programs into independent *modules* with explicit import and export lists. It offers limited facilities for low-level programming and co-routine support; although the *Modula-2* language does not include any input/output routines, there is a standard set of support libraries which are provided with most *Modula-2* compilers. The standard reference text for Modula-2 is [17].

Pop-11

A language combining some of the features of Lisp with a more familiar-looking syntax, popular in Britain in the artificial intelligence community. The original version, *Pop-2*, was written in assembler for Versions 6 and 7 on the PDP11; *Pop-11* is based on an abstract machine plus an interpreter. Whereas *Pop-2* was a programming language, *Pop-11* is a programming environment which comes complete with its own editor (*ved*) and an on-line help system and allows the user to mix routines written in *Pop-11*, *Prolog* and *Lisp*.

Prolog

A logic-based language, likely to be extensively used in the "5th generation" projects developing advanced man-machine interfaces on powerful new hardware architectures. There are several versions, including CProlog from the University of Edinburgh, for the VAX.

Snobol

A string manipulation language. Some Bell Laboratories distributions include an interpreter for SNOBOL3, but (surprisingly, since the language originated there), not its more widespread successor SNOBOL4. Spitbol, an extension of SNOBOL4, is available for the VAX.

C++

The programming discipline known as *Object-Oriented Programming* is becoming progressively more popular, and a variety of object-oriented languages is becoming available. The object-oriented language that is most often available under Unix is *C++*, designed by Bjarne Stroustrup of Bell Laboratories. It is described in detail in [16].

12.3 LANGUAGE IMPLEMENTATION TOOLS

For those who wish to implement their own languages Unix offers two invaluable tools, *lex* and *yacc*. *lex* generates C code to break up an input stream into separate items, given a description of the items in a notation similar to the regular expressions used by *ex*. It can be used in many applications, but is particularly useful for producing the *lexical analysis* component of a language compiler or interpreter. *yacc* ("Yet Another Compiler-Compiler") takes a description of a grammar, and produces code to analyse the corresponding language. It is designed to work hand in hand with *lex*, and is frequently used on Unix for writing programming language *syntax analysers*.

12.4 DATABASE MANAGEMENT SYSTEMS

As Unix becomes ever more popular as an environment for business users, a number of *database management systems* have become available. Many of these are based on the *relational model*. A *relation* is in essence a 2-dimensional table, such as

Serial Number	Description	Manufacturer	Model Number	Room
A464	Vacuum cleaner	Numatic	VC250	10.40
A478	Computer	Apple	II Plus	9.1g
A479	Terminal	Lear Siegler	ADM5	9.3c
A480	Terminal	Lear Siegler	ADM3A	9.3c
A491	Graph Plotter	H-P	7221C	7.1b
A533	Computer	BBC	B	9.11
A591	X11 Terminal	NCD	A	3.11

which might form part of an inventory listing. A *relational database* is a collection of relations, and a Database Management System (*DBMS*) provides the means of examining and updating their contents, and creating new databases.

The oldest Unix DBMS is *ingres*, a relational database system developed at the University of California at Berkeley to run on the PDP-11. Versions of *ingres* are now available for many versions of Unix and many processor families, including VAX, Motorola 68000, Intel 80386 and others. It is a large package, and imposes a significant load even on a powerful machine such as the VAX, but offers in compensation a comprehensive relational database management system.

An alternative relational database system is *Oracle*, which provides similar performance to *ingres* and is available on an almost equal range of equipment. The designers of *Oracle* claim that it works particularly well in multiple-processor Unix systems, such as those made by Pyramid and Sequent.

One slightly unusual alternative in the arena of database management systems is *Pick*, designed by Richard Pick. *Pick* is not simply a DBMS but is an entire operating system which supports a highly efficient relation-based file store together with a command language to manipulate the relations. Although *Pick* was designed to run alone, systems are becoming available in which Unix and *Pick* operate side-by-side, offering a business user the software tools of Unix and the relational database management power of *Pick*.

In many data management problems the use of *ingres*, *Oracle* or a similar DBMS may save much effort in building special-purpose application programs, as well as providing scope for unanticipated extensions to the original system.

Chapter 13

Communications and Networking

In this chapter we explore some of the facilities available in Unix to support computer networks — that is, groups of machines connected together and capable of sharing information. The connections between the machines can vary widely in speed, from *Ethernet* at ten million bits per second to *RS232* at ten thousand bits per second or less. We divide the discussion into three sections — *communications*, covering low speed and long distance data connections, *inter-process communication*, which provides many of the facilities upon which networking is based, and *networking*, covering short distance and high speed connections.

13.1 COMMUNICATIONS

There is a variety of communications software now available for Unix systems. Probably the best known and most widely used is the *uucp* family of programs. The chief member of this family is *uucp* (Unix to Unix Copy) itself. *uucp* provides a mechanism for transferring files between Unix systems which are connected by any sort of communications line. The most common forms of connection are telephone line (with autodialler and modems) or just ordinary terminal lines connected together "back to back", but *uucp* can also use *Ethernet*, *Omninet*, or any other medium.

uucp behaves almost exactly like *cp*, except that pathnames may be extended by appending the name of a different system on to the front followed by an exclamation mark, the local file (if it is being sent) will be copied to a spool directory, and the copy to the remote system will not normally occur immediately. For example:

```
$  uucp myfile.here othervax!/usr/pg/jim/myfile.there
```
Copy from local to distant system
```
$  uucp perq1!program.c program.c
```
Copy from distant system to local
```
$  uucp perq1!booklist perq2!booklist
```
Copy between two distant systems

Of course, you must be authorised to use any other systems which you access through *uucp*. Related to *uucp* is *uux*, which executes a shell command on some other computer system.

An alternative communications package, offering facilities similar to those of *uucp*, is *unet*, produced by 3COM Corporation. This is in many ways a more advanced system than *uucp*, better designed for making use of fast local-area network hardware.

Rather than the delayed transfers and command execution provided by *uucp*, you may want to connect your terminal "through" the local system to some other, as though you were connected to it directly. The standard program *cu* ("Call Unix") can be used for this on AT&T Unix systems; the program *tip* is often provided on Berkeley Unix systems. In addition to connecting you to another Unix system, *cu* and *tip* can handle simple file transfers and execution of commands on your local system. Similar programs have been developed with the capability of connecting to and transferring files between machines running any operating system which can be described in a simple table, for example *call* (developed at the University of Leeds) and *link* (Queen Mary College, London).

The file transfer protocol called *kermit* is beginning to appear on many Unix systems — it has the advantage of being a protocol that can be implemented on a wide variety of machines, over a wide variety of networks. The packet-based *kermit* protocols are clearly defined in the manual by Frank da Cruz ([5]); as a result, many implementations of *kermit* are available for a wide variety of machines. Many *kermit* implementations include a "terminal emulator" for interactive sessions. One of the major benefits of the *kermit* protocol is its robust design; it can be used over non-transparent networks on which certain control characters are trapped and handled by the network.

As an alternative to communicating over telephone and leased lines, many medium to large-scale computer installations are beginning to use the *X.25* family of protocols for long-distance communication. The X.25 protocols support a *packet network*, in which a large number of sites are connected to a common network; when a data packet is sent into the network, the destination address is included in the packet — it is then the responsibility of the network to find a route by which to send the data packet. Many national telephone companies provide a public network based around X.25; in the United Kingdom, British Telecom provide the *PSS* (Packet Switch Service) and *IPSS* (International PSS) services. There are a number of academic networks based around X.25, for example *JANET* (the UK-based Joint Academic Network), *EARN* (the European Academic Research Network) and *Bitnet*; these networks are usually based on leased communication lines, with privately-owned X.25 equipment. Although X.25 networks are often quite expensive to use, they have the benefit of running at higher speed than conventional telephone lines and providing an error-free service.

13.2 INTER-PROCESS COMMUNICATION

Before we discuss networking, we will discuss *inter-process communication*, since the facilities provided by *IPC* underpin most of the facilities provided by networking. Different flavours of Unix provide different flavours of *IPC*, but all of the flavours set out to provide a similar facility — to allow the programmer to send and receive messages between two or more processes. Sometimes the processes are on a single machine; sometimes they are on different machines. The *IPC* mechanisms that we will discuss here are *pipes*, *named pipes*, *shared memory*, *semaphores*, *sockets* and *streams*. The first of these, the *pipe*, is the IPC facility that is available on all flavours of Unix.

Pipes

A *pipe* is a *shared queue* for passing data between Unix processes; it is visible to the Unix programmer as a pair of *file descriptors*, one of which will allow writing and the other, reading. One of the basic limitations of the pipe is that the processes that access the pipe must have a common *parent process* — that is, both processes must have been created by a single process which created the pipe and then *forked* to create the communicating processes; this is a severe limitation.

When processes are connected *via* a pipe, the reading process can accept data by reading from one end of the pipe while the writing process writes to the other end — neither process need worry about the amount of data that is being transferred, since Unix will buffer the data and synchronise the processes. The only limitation is the maximum size of the pipe — if the writing process attempts to write too much data into the pipe it will "block" (be unable to continue) until the reading process removes at least some of the contents of the pipe. The maximum size of a pipe is system dependent — on many systems, it is 4096 bytes.

If a process attempts to read from an empty pipe, it will "block" until something is written into the pipe; if a process attempts to write to a pipe after the reading end has been closed, it will be sent a *signal.*

Named Pipes

As a partial solution to the common-parent problem with pipes, many versions of Unix (particularly those versions derived from AT&T Unix), provide *named pipes* or *FIFO*'s (for First In, First Out). A named pipe appears as a file in the Unix file space. Applying the *ls* command to a directory containing a named pipe will produce something like:

```
$  ls -l
total 34
-rwxr-xr-x 1 User      12728 May 1 12:29 a.out
prw-r----- 1 User          0 May 2 13:54 fifo
-rw-r--r-- 1 Another      84 May 1 12:29 prog.c
drwxr-xr-x 2 User         32 May 1 12:29 subd1
drwxr-xr-x 2 User         32 May 1 12:29 subd2
```

The second file listed, "fifo", is marked with the letter *p* indicating that it is a *pipe.* Named pipes are created using the *mknod* command or the *mknod* system call; once they have been created they will remain in existence until they are explicitly removed.

Once a named pipe has been created, two processes can use it to communicate by one process opening the pipe for reading while another process opens the pipe for writing; the reading process will "block" until the writing process sends some data; any amount of data can be sent, and each read/write operation can be of any size. When the writing process closes the pipe, the reading process sees an *end-of-file* condition. Unlike conventional pipes, writing to a named pipe which has not been opened for reading (or has been closed) will not result in a signal—the writing process will simply "block".

Shared Memory

If two processes need to share a relatively small amount of information, in the region of 4096 bytes to 8192 bytes, some versions of Unix allow them to use *shared memory.* (There are a number of different versions of this technique; we will describe the System V.3 AT&T version.) If a process wishes to create a section of memory which is to be *shared,* it uses the *shmget* system call. This creates an area of shared memory and assigns a unique identifier to the newly created areas. The programmer can then use the (delightfully named) *shmctl, shmop, shmat* and *shmdt* system calls to manipulate the memory area or to attach it to a process.

It is important to understand that a shared memory area, once created, is quite independent of the process that created it — the creating process can exit without affecting the shared area. Shared memory areas only disappear when they are deleted (using *shmctl*), or when the machine is shut down.

Semaphores

One of the earliest techniques developed for synchronising multiple processes was that of the *semaphore*. A semaphore is simply a variable (usually shown as *mutex* in the literature, for *mutual exclusion*) together with a pair of functions called *send* and *wait*. *Send(mutex)* has the effect of adding one to the value of *mutex*; *wait(mutex)* examines the value of *mutex* — if *mutex* is greater than zero it is decreased by one, otherwise the *waiting* process is suspended until another process calls *send* to increase the value of *mutex*. Despite being rather primitive, semaphores provide an extremely powerful mechanism for synchronising processes. Programmers will quite often use shared memory and semaphores together, to avoid processes colliding over writing to shared memory area.

AT&T Unix provides a set of system calls that implement semaphores. The system call *semget* will create a semaphore and attach a unique identifier to it, in the same manner as *shmget*. *semctl* and *semop* can then be used by a group of co-operating processes.

Sockets

When the University of California at Berkeley began to develop the BSD versions of Unix, one of the aims was to develop a method for interprocess communication between physically separate machines. The network developed by ARPA in the United States had existed for some years when the BSD project began, and it seemed sensible to extend Unix to allow it to be connected to the existing networks; the result was a suite of system calls and library routines that allowed a Berkeley Unix system to be connected to (and to communicate across) the ARPA network.

Systems that are attached to the ARPA network are allocated an *Internet Address* which allows information to be transferred across the network by a variety of routes — the Internet Address of a machine simply serves to identify the machine uniquely without specifying how the machine can be reached. It is then the responsibility of the software that manages the network to find an efficient route to a given machine.

Internet Addresses are four bytes long, and they are expressed in the form *A.B.C.D* where each of *A*, *B*, *C* and *D* is in the range *0..255*, and the protocols that use them are referred to as the *Internet Protocols*. If a computer is attached to the Internet network, it is essential that it should have a unique Internet Address, otherwise chaos would ensue. However, it is quite possible to make use of the Internet protocols without being attached to the Internet — many organisations have their Unix systems connected together in a *Local Area Network*, and make use of the Internet protocols to communicate between the computers within the organisation. In this case, the Internet addresses that are chosen will not matter, since they will never be seen by the outside world; it is only important for each machine within the organisation to have a unique address. The Internet addresses of all the accessible systems will usually be listed on each machine, in a file of the form:

```
192.9.200.1     host1 loghost
192.9.200.2     host2
192.9.200.3     host3
192.9.200.4     host4
192.9.200.5     host5
192.9.200.100   host6
192.9.200.101   host7
```

The Internet address appears on the left, with the name of the machine on the right; any references to the machine named *host5* will be translated by the network software into references to the machine with Internet address *192.9.200.5*. On a conventional Berkeley Unix system this list will appear in a file called */etc/hosts*.

The full details of the Internet Protocols are normally hidden from the user, who may only wish to use an Internet *service* — for example, *remote login* to another computer system, or *file transfer protocol* to move a file from one machine to another across the Internet.

If a programmer wishes to make use of sockets in order to connect two processes together, she must first choose a *service number* that is not occupied. The existing services are usually listed in a file with a format like this:

```
echo      7/udp
ftp       21/tcp
telnet    23/tcp
smtp      25/tcp mail
time      37/udp timserver
# Host specific functions
tftp      69/udp
# UNIX specific services
login     513/tcp
printer   515/tcp
```

The various services provided by the Internet software are listed here by name and number — the login protocol, for example, has service number 513 whereas the simple mail transfer protocol (smtp) has service number 25. These service numbers are used by the Internet software to allow a connection to be made to a corresponding *server* on a machine that can be remote or local. On a conventional Berkeley Unix system this list will appear in a file called */etc/services*.

If a programmer wishes to gain direct access to Berkeley sockets, she must make use of the following Unix library routines:

socket which provides the programmer with access to the network — *socket* does not set up a connection to another system, it simply creates a channel between the programmer and the networking software.

bind which will *bind* an existing socket to an address.

connect which will attempt to connect a socket that has been created (using *socket*) and bound (using *bind*) to another machine. If *connect* is successful, it returns a *file descriptor* which allows the programmer to send and receive data.

listen is applied to a socket that has been created and bound — it informs the networking software that the program is intending to accept incoming connections from *connect* calls on other machines.

accept   will accept an incoming call on a socket that has been created, and
to which *listen* has been applied. Each connection that is attempted,
if accepted, will result in a new file descriptor for the socket.

Berkeley Unix also provides a set of library functions for searching
the Internet host tables for an address, searching the service tables for
a service number and converting addresses between various representations.

Streams

Unlike Berkeley sockets, *streams* were developed by AT&T as a more
general (and, to some extent, more elegant) solution to the problems pre-
sented by *IPC*. A *stream* is a collection of software modules with a *stream
head* connected to a user process and a *driver* connected to a physical
device. Each *stream module* is bi-directional, passing data *downstream*
in the direction of the physical device and *upstream* in the direction of
the user process; the modules within the stream pass *messages* using the
putmsg and *getmsg* system calls. The purpose of streams is to support
multi-layered protocols in an extensible way; it is relatively easy, using
streams, to build up a communications protocol layer by layer, with each
module in the stream handling one layer of the protocol.

Although streams are intended to be an entirely general purpose IPC
mechanism, it is probable that standard modules will be available for connecting user processes *via* local area networks and wide area networks.
Because of the design of streams, it is quite possible for a group of processes to communicate *via* almost any physical medium without any effect on the high-level communications protocol, simply by replacing the
lower-level (downstream) modules.

13.3   NETWORKING

Networking fulfills a number of differing needs; firstly, there is the need
to transfer files from one machine to another in a machine-readable form,
without having interactive access to the remote system; secondly, there
is the need to "log on" to a remote machine and make interactive use of
its facilities without rapid access to any of the files on the local machine
— if files are needed on the remote machine, they can be transferred before the interactive session begins; thirdly, there is *distributed computing,*

where a group of computers will have communal access to a file store. The main purpose of networking is to make the facilities of a group of computers available to a community of users without the users needing to be physically close to any of the computers or any of the file stores.

In this section, we will discuss a number of the facilities that networking, in all its forms, can provide.

File Transfer

The complexity of transferring files between computer systems varies considerably, depending upon the distance between the machines, the type of the machines, the network that connects them and the country that you are in.

Transferring files between two Unix systems that are connected via Ethernet is normally quite simple, provided that your version of Unix supports access to the Ethernet. Berkeley Unix provides the *ftp* (File Transfer) protocol which is described in a publication from SRI International [1]; this protocol sits above the TCP/IP communications protocols provided by most implementations of Berkeley Unix, and documented in [3].

Tranferring files over a Wide-Area Network depends heavily on the country that you are in and your network connections; in the U.S.A., you may have access to the Internet which supports a wide-area network running the TCP/IP family of protocols; in Europe or the U.K., you may have access to one of the academic research networks (such as JANET or EARN), or you may be able to access one of the commercial networks based upon X.25 such as PSS or IPSS. If you do not have access to any of these networks, it should be possible for you to use the public telephone network, together with a modem and a copy of *uucp*.

Remote Login

Remote Login provides you with the ability to connect to, and log in to, a physically remote machine — it may be in the next office, or it may be several thousand kilometres away. Remote login, like file transfer, is very dependent on the type of network to which you have access. Many of the networks based upon TCP/IP and X.25 provide remote login facilities in addition to file transfer; Berkeley Unix provides two programs for remote login, one of them called *telnet* (based upon the protocol published by SRI International [2]), and one of them called *rlogin*. *telnet* is a widely accepted Internet standard which is designed to allow you log on to a remote machine with a different operating system; *rlogin* assumes that you are logging in to another Unix system, and exchanges information about your environment (what sort of terminal you are using, your username, etc.) with the remote machine.

Many networks based around X.25 provide a remote login protocol, although the details of the protocol vary between networks. In general, an X.25 network is accessed using a *PAD* (Packet Assembler and Disassembler) which can be implemented in a mixture of hardware and software.

If you do not have access to a network that can provide any of these protocols, you can usually gain access to another system by using the public telephone network, a modem and a copy of *cu* or *tip*.

Distributed File Stores

In recent years with the appearance of very fast local-area networks such as ethernet, token ring and fibre-optic ring there has been a steady increase in the appearance of *distributed file stores* for a wide variety of computer systems.

The Newcastle Connection

The set of protocols known as *The Newcastle Connection* was one of the first distributed file stores, and was developed by the University of Newcastle-upon-Tyne in England. This system completely disguises the existence of a network from the user, who merely sees that the local file system tree is now attached to a larger tree, as though mounted on it. This larger tree comprises the file systems of all accessible Unix systems. The file store of a remote machine is made visible by attaching it to the file store of the local machine above the level of "/" (the root directory). On a conventional Unix system the parent of the root directory is defined to be the root directory; on a Unix system which supports the Newcastle Connection, the parent of the root directory is a directory which contains the names of all the accessible machines. Each remote machine is normally allocated a unique name which is used to label the root of its file store.

For example, if you wanted to copy a number of files between a number of connected systems you would enter:

```
$   cd /
$   cp /tmp/myfile.here \
            ../othervax/usr/pg/jim/myfile.there
$   cp ../orion1/program.c /tmp/program.c
$   cp ../orion1/booklist ../orion2/booklist
```

Network File Store

Developed by Sun Microsystems, *NFS* differs considerably from the New-castle Connection in that *sections* of the filestore of one machine can be mounted on another machine; NFS is described as a *stateless* protocol, which means that the *server* (the machine supplying the files) does not record any state information about the *client* (the machine that is accessing the files). In other words, when a client program opens a file on a server all the information relating to that open file is held on the client.

The major benefit of a stateless protocol is its robust nature — if a server machine fails, the clients need only wait for the server to recover; since no state information is held on the server, no state information is lost if the server fails. This makes error recovery considerably simpler. State-less protocols have two major disadvantages; the first is that file locking becomes much more complex — if two machines wish to co-operate in writing to a file they must negotiate directly, rather than relying upon the server system to prevent them from writing to the file simultaneously; the second disadvantage of stateless protocols is that they make it almost impossible to access remote devices, since devices carry a considerable amount of state information while you are using them. One possible so-lution to the file-locking problem is to implement a *lock server* process which runs on the server machine and intercepts requests from clients; when it receives a request from a client for a file to be locked, it issues a lock request on the server machine. Although such a protocol alleviates the file locking problem, it complicates error recovery in the event of the server failing.

Despite the drawbacks inherent in NFS, it has been widely accepted by many manufacturers as a *de facto* standard; it is available on a wide range of architectures, from IBM PC compatibles up to large mainframe systems. The conclusion appears to be that NFS offers considerable per-formance and functionality at the expense of modifying the semantics of the Unix file store.

Remote File Store

Unlike NFS, the *Remote File Store* (or *RFS*) designed at AT&T provides state information on the server machine. Unlike NFS, it is able to support access from a client system to the physical devices on a server machine. As a result, it models the semantics of the Unix file store much more closely than NFS at the expense of making error recovery considerably more complicated — if an RFS server fails, all clients with open files must take appropriate action to re-synchronise themselves with the server.

13.4 GRAPHICAL DISPLAYS

As mentioned at the end of Chapter 7, window management systems have been available for some time on high-performance workstations — some supporting Unix, some supporting proprietary operating systems. Such window management systems have, in the past, been based upon protocols that were specific to one manufacturer, making it difficult for users to attach alternative graphical displays to such a system. In addition, there was no clear demarcation between the workstation and the graphics engine — in many cases the display memory of the graphics engine was accessed directly by the workstation, making it extremely difficult to separate physically the workstation and the display.

However, two recent events are leading to a major shift in the way in which multi-user computer systems are accessed; one event is the rapid reduction in the cost of large, high-speed memory devices; the other event is the appearance of standard protocols for communicating graphical operations over medium- to high-speed networks.

As a result of these events, it is becoming possible for graphical displays to be sited remotely from the computer that drives them. It is no longer necessary for the host computer to have direct access to the display memory of the graphical display, thus allowing a single host computer to support a number of such displays. This has led to the appearance of low-cost desk-top display systems that are designed to run attached to a remote host *via* a local-area network. The graphical protocol that is used to communicate commands between the host and the workstation is quite often the X11 protocol, although the NeWS (Network Extensible Window System) from Sun Microsystems is slowly gaining in popularity.

13.5 THE Unix NETWORK

Many Unix sites in the U.S.A. are linked by the *usenet* electronic mail and news network. European sites have access to this network through *eunet*, which is based at the Mathematics Centre, Amsterdam; most sites in the United Kingdom contact *eunet* through the University of Kent. These networks provide rapid dissemination of news (and jokes, recipes, film reviews and other detritus) through the Unix community. They also provide an electronic mail service to other networks, such as ARPAnet (Advanced Research Projects Agency network) or NSFnet (National Science Foundation network). The minimum requirement to join is a modem attached to your computer so that a site on the network can dial you up at occasional intervals, together with enough funds to pay your share of the telephone calls required.

Appendix A

Unix Commands

The following table lists all of the commands that are likely to be found on recent versions of AT&T Unix (System V.2 or later) and recent versions of Berkeley Unix (BSD4.2 or later). The section number in parenthesis refers to the manual section where the command is described. Suffices on the section number are:

 c   Related to communications

 g   Graphics

 m   Systems management commands

An entry of "sh" as the section means that the command is described under *sh(1)*.

Most commands in Section 6 are games; many distributions of Unix omit these.

Command	Summary
.(sh)	Read commands
:(sh)	Comment
ac(1m)	Accounting
accton(1m)	Accounting on/off
adb(1)	Debugger
ar(1)	Library maintenance
arcv(1m)	Convert *ar* file
arithmetic(6)	Number drill
as(1)	Assembler
at(1)	Schedule command
awk(1)	Pattern-processing
backgammon(6)	Board game
banner(6)	Print large
basename(1)	Remove suffix
bc(1)	Arithmetic language
bcd(6)	Binary-coded decimal

Command	Summary
bj(6)	Blackjack (pontoon)
break(sh)	Exit from loop
cal(1)	Print calendar
calendar(1)	Diary reminder
case(sh)	Multi-way condition
cat(1)	Concatenate files
cb(1)	C pretty-printer
cc(1)	C compiler
cd(1)	Change directory
checkeq(1)	Check *eqn* input
chess(6)	Chess
chgrp(1)	Change group
chmod(1)	Change protection
chown(1)	Change owner
clri(1m)	Clear i-node
cmp(1)	Compare files
col(1)	Filter reverse motions
colcrt(1)	Filter all control codes
comm(1)	Common lines
continue(sh)	Loop again
cp(1)	Copy file
cpio(1)	Copy files to/from magnetic tape
csplit(1)	Split up file
cu(1c)	Call up Unix
cubic(6)	3D TicTacToe
cut(1)	Extract columns
date(1)	Print/set date/time
dc(1)	Desk calculator
dcheck(1m)	Check consistency
dd(1)	Convert file
deroff(1)	Remove *nroff* constructs
df(1m)	Report free space
diff(1)	File comparison
diff3(1)	3-way comparison
dircmp(1)	Compare directories
du(1)	Report disk usage
dump(1m)	File-system archive
dumpdir(1m)	List *dump* tape

Command	Summary
echo(1)	Print arguments
ed(1)	Editor
egrep(1)	Find pattern
enroll(1)	Join secret mail
eqn(1)	Format mathematics
eval(sh)	Evaluate command
exec(sh)	Overlay command
exit(sh)	Exit
export(sh)	Add to environment
expr(1)	Evaluate arguments
f77(1)	Fortran 77
factor(1)	Factorise number
false(1)	Do nothing, fail
fgrep(1)	Fast *grep*
file(1)	Identify file-type
find(1)	Traverse tree
fold(1)	Fold lines
for(sh)	Loop
fortune(6)	Print epigram
graph(1g)	Draw graph
grep(1)	Find pattern
hangman(6)	Word game
head(1)	Beginning of a file
icheck(1m)	Check filesystem
if(sh)	Condition
iostat(1m)	Report I/O stats
join(1)	Database operator
kill(1)	Send signal
ld(1)	Loader
learn(1)	Teach Yourself
lex(1)	Lexical-analyser generator
lint(1)	De-fluff C programs
ln(1)	Link file
login(1)	Log on to Unix
look(1)	Find lines
lookbib(1)	Bibliographic retrieval
lorder(1)	Order object library
lpr(1)	Printer spooler

Command	Summary
ls(1)	Directory listing
m4(1)	Macroprocessor
mail(1)	Send/receive mail
make(1)	Maintain program files
man(1)	Print manual pages
mesg(1)	Permit/deny messages
mkdir(1)	Make directory
mkfs(1m)	Make file-system
mknod(1m)	Make special file
mount(1m)	Mount file-system
mv(1)	Rename file
ncheck(1m)	Map i-nums to names
neqn(1)	Format mathematics
newgrp(1)	Change group
nice(1)	Low priority command
nm(1)	Print symbol table
nohup(1)	Interrupt-immune command
nroff(1)	Text formatter
od(1)	Octal dump
passwd(1)	Change password
paste(1)	Vertical 'cat'
pc(1)	**Pascal** compiler
pcc(1)	Portable C compiler
plot(1g)	Graph-plotting
pr(1)	Print file
primes(1)	Generate primes
prof(1)	Execution profiler
ps(1)	Process status
pstat(1m)	System status
ptx(1)	Permuted index
pwd(1)	Working directory
quot(1m)	File-system usage
ranlib(1)	Make library random-access
ratfor(1)	FORTRAN preprocessor
read(sh)	Read variable
readonly(sh)	Protect variable
refer(1)	Bibliography processor
restor(1m)	Restore from tape

Command	Summary
rev(1)	Reverse lines
reversi(6)	Othello
rm(1)	Remove file
rmdir(1)	Remove directory
roff(1)	Text formatter
sa(1m)	System accounting
sed(1)	Stream editor
set(sh)	Set option
sh(1)	Bourne Shell
shift(sh)	Shift arguments
size(1)	Object module size
sleep(1)	Suspend execution
sort(1)	Sort/merge files
spell(1)	Check spelling
spellin(1)	Add to dictionary
spellout(1)	Check dictionary
spline(1g)	Curve-fitting
split(1)	Split file
strip(1)	Remove name list
struct(1)	Structure FORTRAN
stty(1)	Set/report terminal settings
su(1)	Substitute user ID
sum(1)	Checksum file
sync(1)	Do pending output
tabs(1)	Set tab stops
tail(1)	Print end of file
tar(1)	Tape archiver
tbl(1)	Format tables
tc(1)	Display *troff* on Tektronix
tee(1)	T-junction
test(1)	Test condition
time(1)	Report execution time
times(sh)	Report process time
tk(1)	Tektronix paginator
touch(1)	Access file
tr(1)	Translate chars
trap(sh)	Catch interrupts
troff(1)	Typeset text

Command	Summary
true(1)	Do nothing, succeed
tty(1)	Terminal name
umask(sh)	Set file mask
umount(1m)	Unmount file system
uniq(1)	Report repeated lines
units(1)	Unit conversion
uucp(1c)	Unix to Unix copy
uulog(1c)	*Uucp* log
uux(1c)	Remote command
wait(1)	Wait for process
wall(1m)	Broadcast message
wc(1)	Word count
while(sh)	Loop
who(1)	Who is logged on
write(1)	Talk to logged-on user
xget(1)	Read secret mail
xsend(1)	Send secret mail
yacc(1)	Compiler-Compiler

Appendix B

C Library Functions

This is an alphabetic list of all library functions that are available on System V and Berkeley Unix. The number in parentheses is the Manual section where the function is described; a suffix, if any, indicates which library is to be specified to *ld*, as follows:

c	-lcurses	Screen control routines
d	-ldbm	Database routines
m	-lm	Maths Routines
mp	-lmp	Multiple precision arithmetic package
p	-lplot	Plot routines

Entries in Section 2 are mostly system calls: those flagged † are restricted to the super-user; those flagged ‡ form the standard I/O library.

Function	Summary
abort(3)	Die with dump
abs(3)	Absolute value
access(2)	Find permission
acct(2)	† Account on/off
acos(3m)	Arc cosine
addch(3c)	Add character
addstr(3c)	Add string
alarm(2)	Request signal
asctime(3)	Date (string)
asin(3m)	Arc sin
assert(3)	Consistency check
atan(3m)	Arc tangent
atan2(3)	Arc tangent
atof(3)	String to real
atoi(3)	String to int
atol(3)	String to long
attroff(3c)	Attribute off

Function	Summary
attron(3c)	Attribute on
attrset(3c)	Attribute set
box(3c)	Draw a box
brk(2)	Core allocation
cabs(3m)	Complex modulus
calloc(3)	Get zeroed space
ceil(3m)	Int upper bound
chdir(2)	Change directory
chmod(2)	Change mode
chown(2)	† Change owner
chroot(2)	† Change root
circle(3c)	Draw a circle
clearerr(3)	‡ Clear error
close(2)	Close file
copysign(3m)	IEEE arithmetic
cos(3m)	Cosine
cosh(3m)	Hyperbolic cos
creat(2)	Create file
ctime(3)	Date as string
ctype(3)	Character type
curses(3c)	Screen control
dbminit(3d)	Open database
delch(3c)	Delete character
delete(3d)	Delete data
delwin(3c)	Delete window
doupdate(3c)	Update a window
dup(2)	Duplicate descriptor
dup2(2)	Duplicate descriptor
ecvt(3)	Real to string
endgrent(3)	Close group file
endpwent(3)	Close password file
erase(3c)	Erase from a window
execl(2)	Execute program
execle(2)	Execute program
execlp(2)	Execute program
execv(2)	Execute program
execve(2)	Execute program
execvp(2)	Execute program

Function	Summary
_exit(2)	End process
exit(2)	End process
exp(3m)	Exponential
fabs(3m)	Absolute value
fclose(3)	‡ Close stream
fcvt(3)	Real to string
fdopen(3)	‡ Set fileno
feof(3)	‡ End of file
ferror(3)	‡ I/O error
fetch(3d)	Get data by key
fflush(3)	‡ Flush stream
fgetc(3)	‡ Get character
fgets(3)	‡ Read string
fileno(3)	‡ File descriptor
finite(3m)	IEEE arithmetic
firstkey(3d)	Get first key
floor(3m)	Int lower bound
fopen(3)	‡ Open stream
fork(2)	Spawn process
fprintf(3)	‡ Formatted print
fputc(3)	‡ Write character
fputs(3)	‡ Write string
fread(3)	‡ Binary read
free(3)	Free space
freopen(3)	‡ Re-open stream
frexp(3)	Get exponent
fscanf(3)	‡ Formatted read
fseek(3)	‡ Random access
fstat(2)	File status
ftell(3)	‡ Stream pointer
ftime(2)	Date and time
fwrite(3)	‡ Binary write
gcd(3a)	*Mint* gcd
gcvt(3)	Real to string
getc(3)	‡ Get character
getchar(3)	‡ Get character
getegid(2)	Get effective gid
getenv(3)	Get environment

Function	Summary
geteuid(2)	Get effective uid
getgid(2)	Get group ID
getgrent(3)	Get group entry
getgrgid(3)	Get group entry
getgrnam(3)	Get group entry
getlogin(3)	Get login name
getpass(3)	Read password
getpgrp(2)	Get process group
getpid(2)	Get process ID
getpw(3)	Uid to name
getpwent(3)	Get passwd entry
getpwgid(3)	Get passwd entry
getpwnam(3)	Get passwd entry
gets(3)	‡ Read string
getuid(2)	Get user ID
getw(3)	‡ Get word
gmtime(3)	GMT as structure
gtty(2)	Get tty
hypot(3m)	Distance
inch(3c)	Insert a character
index(3)	Char position
initscr(3c)	Initialise screen
ioctl(2)	Device control
isalnum(3)	Character type
isalpha(3)	Character type
isascii(3)	Character type
isatty(3)	Is fd a terminal?
iscntrl(3)	Character type
isdigit(3)	Character type
islower(3)	Character type
isprint(3)	Character type
ispunct(3)	Character type
isspace(3)	Character type
isupper(3)	Character type
itom(3a)	*Int* to *mint*
j0,j1,jn(3m)	Bessel functions
kill(2)	Send signal
l3tol(3)	3-byte int to long

Function	Summary
ldexp(3)	Set mantissa and exponent
link(2)	Make link
localtime(3)	Date as structure
lock(2)	† Lock in memory
log(3m)	Natural log
log10(3m)	Base 10 log
longjmp(3)	Non-local exit
lseek(2)	Random access
ltol3(3)	Long to 3-byte int
madd(3a)	Add *mint*s
malloc(3)	Get space
mdiv(3a)	*Mint* division
min(3a)	*Mint* input
mkdir(2)	Make directory
mknod(2)	† Make special file
mktemp(3)	Make unique name
modf(3)	Split int and fractional part
monitor(3)	Execution profile
mount(2)	† Mount file system
mout(3a)	*Mint* output
msgctl(2)	Message control
msgget(2)	Message get
msgop(2)	Message operation
msgrcv(2)	Message receive
msgsnd(2)	Message send
msqrt(3a)	*Mint* sqrt
msub(3a)	Subtract *mint*s
mult(3a)	*Mint* product
mvcur(3)	Move cursor
nextkey(3d)	Get data key
nice(2)	Set priority
nlist(3)	Get name list
npgrp(2)	Set process group
open(2)	Open file
overlay(3)	Overlay window
pause(2)	Suspend execution
pclose(3)	‡ Close IPC stream
perror(3)	Error message

Function	Summary
pipe(2)	IPC channel
plot(5p)	Plot routines
popen(3)	‡ IPC stream
pow(3m)	Power
pow(3a)	*Mint* power
printf(3)	‡ Formatted print
profil(2)	Execution profile
ptrace(2)	Process trace
putc(3)	‡ Write char
putchar(3)	‡ Write char
puts(3)	‡ Write string
putw(3)	‡ Write word
qsort(3)	Sort
rand(3)	Random number
read(2)	Read from file
realloc(3)	Adjust space
re_comp(3)	Regular expression compiling
re_exec(3)	Regular expression matching
rewind(3)	‡ Reset pointer
rindex(3)	Char position
rpow(3a)	*Mint* power
saveterm(3c)	Save terminal state
sbrk(2)	Get memory
scanf(3)	‡ Formatted read
sdiv(3a)	*Mint* division
setbuf(3)	‡ Assign buffer
setgid(2)	Set group ID
setgrent(3)	Open group file
setjmp(3)	Set non-local exit
setkey(3)	Set encrypt key
setlinebuf(3)	Set line buffering
setpwent(3)	Open passwd file
setuid(2)	Set user ID
shmat(2)	Shared memory attach
shmctl(2)	Shared memory control
shmdt(2)	Shared memory detach
shmget(2)	Shared memory get
shmop(2)	Shared memory operation

Function	Summary
signal(2)	Catch signals
sin(3m)	Sine
sinh(3m)	Hyperbolic sin
sleep(3)	Suspend process
sprintf(3)	‡ Formatted copy
sqrt(3m)	Square root
srand(3)	Initialise *rand*
sscanf(3)	‡ Formatted scan
stat(2)	File status
stime(2)	† Set time
store(3d)	Store by key
strcat(3)	Append string
strcmp(3)	Compare strings
strcpy(3)	Copy string
strlen(3)	String length
strncat(3)	Append string
strncmp(3)	Compare strings
strncpy(3)	Copy string
stty(2)	Set tty
swab(3)	Swap bytes
sync(2)	Do delayed output
system(3)	Shell command
tan(3m)	Tangent
tanh(3m)	Hyperbolic tan
tell(2)	Find file position
time(2)	Date and time
times(2)	Process times
timezone(3)	Name of timezone
tolower(3)	To lower case
toupper(3)	To upper case
traceoff(3c)	Window trace off
traceon(3c)	Window trace on
ttyname(3)	Terminal name
ttyslot(3)	Terminal index
tzset(3)	Set time zone
umask(2)	Set file mask
umount(2)	† Dismount device
ungetc(3)	Unread a char

Function	Summary
unlink(2)	Remove dir entry
utime(2)	Set file times
wait(2)	Wait for termination
write(2)	Write to file
y0,y1,yn(3m)	Bessel functions

Appendix C

---

vi Command Summary

We provide here a summary of *vi* commands. This list is intended to be exhaustive, so not everything that appears in this list is mentioned in the text of Chapter 3.

File Manipulation	
:w	write file
:wq	write file and quit
:q	quit
:q!	quit and discard changes
:e *name*	edit file *name*
:e #	edit alternate file
:n #	edit alternate file
:e +*n*	edit starting at line *n*
:w *name*	write file *name*
:w! *name*	overwrite file *name*
:sh	run shell, then return
:!*cmd*	run command, then return
:n	edit next file in argument list
:n args	specify new argument list
:f	show current file name and line
Positioning Within File	
^F	forward one screen
^B	backward one screen
^D	scroll down half a screen
^U	scroll up half a screen
G	goto line
/*pat*	next line matching *pat*
?*pat*	previous line matching *pat*
n	repeat last / or ?
N	reverse last / or ?
/*pat*/+*n*	n'th line after *pat*

?*pat*?-*n*	n'th line before *pat*
]]	next section or function
[[	previous section or function
%	find matching (,), { or }
Adjusting the Screen	
ˆL	redraw
ˆR	redraw without @ lines
zCR	redraw, current line at top
z-	…at bottom
z.	…at middle
ˆE	scroll up 1 line
ˆY	scroll down 1 line
Line Positioning	
H	Home window line
L	Last window line
M	Middle window line
+	next line, first non-white
-	previous line, first non-white
CR	return, same as +
j or ↓	next line, same column
k or ↑	previous line, same column
Character Positioning	
ˆ	first non-blank
0	beginning of line
$	end of line
h or →	forward
l or ←	backward
ˆH	same as ←
space	same as →
f*x*	find *x* forwards
F*x*	find *x* backwards
t*x*	up to *x* forwards
T*x*	up to *x* backwards
;	repeat last **f**, **F**, **t** or **T**
%	find matching (,), { or }
Words, Sentences, Paragraphs	
w	word forward
b	word backward

e	end of word
)	to next sentence
(	to previous sentence
}	to next paragraph
{	to previous paragraph
W	word delimited by blanks
B	back **W**
E	end of **W**
Insert and Replace	
a	append after cursor
i	insert before cursor
A	append at end of line
I	insert at beginning of line
o	open line above
O	open line below
r*x*	replace single character with *x*
R	replace characters
Corrections During Insertion	
^H	erase last character
^W	erase last word
©	same as ^H
①	erase input line
\	escape an editing character
ESCAPE	end insert mode
^C	interrupt, end insert
^D	backspace over *auto indent*
^V	quote non-printing character
Operators (double to operate in lines)	
d	delete
c	change
>	left shift
<	right shift
!	filter through a command
y	yank lines into a buffer
Yank and Put	
p	put back lines
P	put lines before current line
"*x*p	put from buffer *x*

"xy	yank into buffer x
"xd	delete into buffer x
Marking and Returning	
mx	mark line with letter x
'x	to mark x
'x	...at first non-white
"	previous context
"	...at first non-white
Miscellaneous	
u	undo last change
U	restore current line
.	repeat last edit
"dp	retrieve d'th last delete
C	change rest of current line
D	delete rest of current line
s	substitute characters
S	substitute lines
J	join lines together
x	delete characters
X	...before the cursor
Y	yank lines

Appendix D

A Short History of Unix

There were two main stimuli for the initial development of Unix. The first was the poor response of the time-sharing GECOS system used by Ken Thompson and Dennis Ritchie for their program "space travel", and its physical remoteness (up two flights of stairs!) combined with the fact that a PDP7 was available in close proximity to Thompson's office. This led Thompson and Ritchie to develop a single-user system, coded in assembler, which showed some features ancestral to Unix and used concepts from many other innovative systems, including Multics, CTSS, and CMAS. At first this system was cross-compiled for the PDP 7 on GECOS; before long, however, the effort involved in transporting paper tapes up and down stairs led to the development of a system entirely resident on the PDP 7; this system included the *fork* primitive, and would support two users, but pipes and the tree-structured file system were yet to come.

The second stimulus was the requirement within AT&T's Bell Laboratories for a text processing system. This was to be implemented on a PDP11/20, and it was decided to implement Unix, which had by now been so named[1] by Brian Kernighan, on the PDP11 to support this project. The first PDP11 version, still written in assembler, now included the familiar file system and a command interface which bore many of the features of the Version 6 shell, the first destined to become widespread outside Bell Laboratories. The vintage of this version is well illustrated by giving the etymology of the interactive delete command *dsw*. This utility, "delete with switches", was among the very earliest Unix programs written and originally the user showed whether she wanted a file deleted by setting the front-panel switches on the PDP7.

Pipes appeared in the next version of the system, and use of a high-level language (B, a derivative of BCPL) was explored. This led to a version in which many of the utilities were coded in an early form of C,

---

[1]The name has been scurrilously explained as describing "a castrated version of Multics"

224

and eventually to a version with the kernel itself coded almost entirely in C.

A major re-write of the system, leading to the very popular Version 7, resulted from a project by Thompson and Ritchie to transport Unix to different hardware, the Interdata 8/32. This project led to extensions in the file system, the command interface, and C itself, and the resulting code was highly portable, with hardware-dependencies kept to a minimum, and clearly identified.

At this time, DEC's VAX was becoming very popular, particularly in the academic environment in which Unix was now well established. Bell Laboratories produced a version for it called 32V; this version never found particular favour, notably because it did not exploit paging, and VAX users instead turned to the versions developed under ARPA (later DARPA) contract at the University of California at Berkeley. Of these versions, number 4.2 enjoyed enormous popularity and many flavours of Unix current today are referred to as "4.2bsd derivatives". The Berkeley developments were responsible for many of the features and utilities of today's Unix, notably *vi*, the C-Shell and sockets.

During this time AT&T continued major development, producing in 1981 a version oriented toward commercial exploitation called *System III* and, more recently in 1983, *System V Release 1* (System IV never saw the light of day!). These versions represent another major thread in Unix development — features in System V Release 3 that are not found in pure Berkeley derivatives are shared memory, *streams* (the IPC mechanism used instead of sockets), and *RFS*, Remote File Sharing, a mechanism for sharing files across systems analogous to Sun's NFS. In 1985 AT&T produced the System V Interface Definition, pronounced *SVID* which was a serious attempt to standardise the appearance of future Unix systems. There are many differences, some cosmetic and some fundamental, between 4.2bsd and System V; some Unix systems will offer just one or the other, while others will back both horses by making the capabilities of both available — the Sun operating system and DEC's Ultrix are examples of this, and represent an enthusiasm for some convergent development in the future.

By the mid-eighties many companies had become interested in providing their own version of Unix — at the time of writing (1990) no major vendor is outside the Unix market. The fact that Unix was becoming a *de facto* standard had not gone unnoticed by these vendors, who were understandably unhappy at the prospect of AT&T being allowed to corner the market by specifying a Unix standard with the SVID. As a result, a number of loose-knit co-operations have developed between many companies, ostensibly so that they may develop a common system to the benefit of the customer: The cynic might feel that such co-operation has more to do with inter-company rivalry and politics, and a fear of being left out of a very profitable market. This book is not the place to document the evolution of these organisms (an evolution which is in any case far from complete) but the interested reader will encounter in the computer press reference to *X/Open*, an alliance originally of European companies who were later joined by, among others, DEC, Sun and AT&T; to *POSIX*, a true standard laid down by the IEEE defining a portable operating system interface for computing environments; to *OSF*, the Open Software Foundation, formed as a non-profit making company including IBM among its original sponsors, that is dedicated to developing a standard, vendor independent operating system; and most recently to *Unix International*, (known in a slightly earlier incarnation as the Archer Group) which seems to have very similar aims, and notably includes among its membership AT&T and Sun. These two groupings are the current major rivals in deciding the way forward. If the reader finds this potted genealogy confusing, this is not in the least surprising. Being specific may well not be of any value since there is nothing to suggest that the formation (and demise) of these alliances has finished, or (at the time of writing) that they have settled on the shape of things to come, although the next major evolutionary step, the full release of System V Release 4 by AT&T (and therefore with the support of Unix International), promises all the features of earlier System V versions, *and* the Berkeley enhancements *and* compatibility with Xenix, which arguably represents yet another strand of development in the whole business.

The rough chronology of this development is summarised in Table D.1. This table omits (for clarity!) the releases of operating systems by such major players in the game as Sun (SunOS Version 4.0.3, 1989) and DEC (Ultrix Version 3.0, 1989).

1969	Initial PDP7 version
1970	2-user PDP7 version; name "Unix" coincd; PDP11/20 system started
1971	First Edition for PDP11 produced
1972	Second Edition (including pipes)
1973	Rewritten in C
1975	Sixth Edition made available to academic users at very small fee
1977-1978	Unix ported to Interdata 8/32
1979	Seventh Edition released
1980	32V (for the VAX) released by AT&T
1980	Version 3.2bsd (for the VAX) released by Berkeley
1981	System III released by AT&T
1983	System V.1 released by AT&T
1984	Version 4.2bsd released by Berkeley
1985	System V.2 released by AT&T
1985	SVID published by AT&T
1986	Version 4.3bsd released by Berkeley
1986	System V.3 released by AT&T
1987	SVID (Issue 2) published by AT&T
1990	System V.4 and SVID (Issue 3) promised

Table D.1: An Abbreviated Chronology of Unix

Appendix E

Trademarks

The text makes many references to words which are trademarks; these are listed below. We apologise for any omissions or errors in the list, and shall be glad to incorporate corrections in any future edition.

AUX	Apollo
BASIC-PLUS	Digital Equipment Corporation
CP/M	Digital Research
Coherent	Mark Williams Inc.
Cromix	Cromemco Ltd.
DEC	Digital Equipment Corporation
Ethernet	Xerox Corporation
Eunice	Stanford Research Institute
GNU	Free Software Foundation
HP-UX	Hewlett Packard Corporation
Idris	Whitesmiths Ltd.
MACH	Carnegie Mellon University
MC68000	Motorola Inc.
MINIX	Andrew Tanenbaum
MV	Data General
Netix	Bell Telephone Manufacturing Co.
NeWS	Sun Microsystems Ltd.
NFS	Sun Microsystems Ltd.
ONIX	ONYX Systems Inc.
PDP	Digital Equipment Corporation
PNX	International Computers Ltd.
Perq	Three Rivers Inc.
PostScript	Adobe Systems Inc.
Pixel	Instrumentation Laboratories
RFS	Bell Laboratories
RT11	Digital Equipment Corporation
SUNOS	Sun Microsystems Ltd.

System V	Bell Laboratories
Teletype	Teletype Corporation
TNIX	Tektronix
Tower	NCR Corporation
UCSD	SofTech
UNET	3COM Corporation
UNIX	Bell Laboratories
UNOS	Charles River Corporation
UN/VS	Data General
UTS	Amdahl Corporation
UniFlex	TSC
Uniplus	Heurika
Unity	Human Computing Resources
X11	MIT
VAX	Digital Equipment Corporation
VM470	International Business Machines
VMS	Digital Equipment Corporation
Xenix	Microsoft Corporation
Z80	Zilog
Zeus	Zilog

Bibliography

[1] *RFC959*. SRI International, 1979.

[2] *RFC854*. SRI International, 1980.

[3] *RFC791*. SRI International, 1981.

[4] M. Bach. *The Design of The Unix Operating System*. Prentice-Hall International, 1986.

[5] Frank da Cruz. *Kermit: A File Transfer Protocol*. Digital Press, 1987.

[6] Ralph E. Griswold and Madge T. Griswold. *The Icon Programming Language*. Prentice-Hall Inc., Englewood Cliffs, New Jersey, 1983.

[7] Brian W. Kernighan and L.L. Cherry. A system for typesetting mathematics, 1979. neqn eqn.

[8] Brian W. Kernighan and M.D. McIlroy (editors). *Unix Programmer's Manual, 7th Edition*. Bell Telephone Laboratories, Inc., Murray Hill, NJ, 1979.

[9] Brian W. Kernighan and Dennis M. Ritchie. *The C Programming Language*. Prentice-Hall International, 1978.

[10] Brian W. Kernighan and Dennis M. Ritchie. *The C Programming Language*. Prentice-Hall International, 1988.

[11] M.E. Lesk. Tbl - a program to format tables, 1979.

[12] M.E. Lesk. Typing documents on the unix system: Using the -ms macros with nroff and troff, 1979.

[13] M.E. Lesk. Updating publication lists, 1979.

[14] J.F. Ossanna. Nroff/troff user's manual, 1979.

[15] Martin Richards and Colin Whitby-Strevens. *BCPL: The Language and its Compiler*. Cambridge University Press, 1980.

[16] Bjarne Stroustrup. *The C++ Programming Language*. Addison-Wesley, 1986.

[17] Niklaus Wirth. *Programming in Modula-2*. Springer-Verlag, 1985.

Index